ZERO DAY

NOVICE NO MORE

EXPOSE SOFTWARE VULNERABILITIES AND ELIMINATE BUGS

4 BOOKS IN 1

BOOK 1
ZERO DAY DEMYSTIFIED: A BEGINNER'S GUIDE TO UNCOVERING
SOFTWARE VULNERABILITIES

BOOK 2
ZERO DAY EXPOSED: INTERMEDIATE TECHNIQUES FOR IDENTIFYING AND
PATCHING SOFTWARE BUGS

BOOK 3
MASTERING ZERO DAY: ADVANCED STRATEGIES FOR VULNERABILITY
DISCOVERY AND REMEDIATION

BOOK 4
ZERO DAY UNLEASHED: EXPERT-LEVEL TACTICS FOR EXPLOITING AND
PROTECTING AGAINST SOFTWARE VULNERABILITIES

ROB BOTWRIGHT

Published by Rob Botwright
Library of Congress Cataloging-in-Publication Data
ISBN 978-1-83938-555-1
Cover design by Rizzo

Disclaimer

The contents of this book are based on extensive research and the best available historical sources. However, the author and publisher make no claims, promises, or guarantees about the accuracy, completeness, or adequacy of the information contained herein. The information in this book is provided on an "as is" basis, and the author and publisher disclaim any and all liability for any errors, omissions, or inaccuracies in the information or for any actions taken in reliance on such information.

The opinions and views expressed in this book are those of the author and do not necessarily reflect the official policy or position of any organization or individual mentioned in this book. Any reference to specific people, places, or events is intended only to provide historical context and is not intended to defame or malign any group, individual, or entity.

The information in this book is intended for educational and entertainment purposes only. It is not intended to be a substitute for professional advice or judgment. Readers are encouraged to conduct their own research and to seek professional advice where appropriate.

Every effort has been made to obtain necessary permissions and acknowledgments for all images and other copyrighted material used in this book. Any errors or omissions in this regard are unintentional, and the author and publisher will correct them in future editions.

Introduction

In today's digitally connected world, where technology underpins nearly every aspect of our lives, the importance of cybersecurity cannot be overstated. As our reliance on software systems and applications continues to grow, so does the need to safeguard them from the ever-present threat of vulnerabilities and exploits. Enter the world of "ZERO DAY: Novice No More" – a comprehensive book bundle designed to empower individuals on their journey from novices to experts in the realm of software vulnerability discovery and remediation.

The "ZERO DAY: Novice No More" bundle comprises four meticulously crafted books, each tailored to a specific stage of the learning journey. Whether you're taking your first steps into the world of cybersecurity or seeking to master the most advanced strategies, this bundle has something to offer every aspiring cybersecurity professional.

Book 1: "ZERO DAY DEMYSTIFIED: A Beginner's Guide to Uncovering Software Vulnerabilities" serves as the starting point for novices. In this book, we demystify the complex world of software vulnerabilities, breaking down jargon and concepts into easily digestible pieces. Novices will learn the fundamentals of identifying, understanding, and addressing software vulnerabilities, laying a solid foundation for their future cybersecurity endeavors.

Building upon this foundation, Book 2: "ZERO DAY EXPOSED: Intermediate Techniques for Identifying and Patching Software Bugs" introduces intermediate techniques that bridge the gap between basic understanding and comprehensive expertise. Readers will delve deeper into the intricacies of software vulnerabilities, exploring advanced methods for their detection and mitigation.

In Book 3: "MASTERING ZERO DAY: Advanced Strategies for Vulnerability Discovery and Remediation," readers will ascend to the ranks of advanced practitioners. This book unveils cutting-edge strategies and methodologies employed by cybersecurity experts. Here, you will discover how to tackle even the most challenging vulnerabilities with confidence and precision.

The culmination of this journey awaits in Book 4: "ZERO DAY UNLEASHED: Expert-Level Tactics for Exploiting and Protecting Against Software Vulnerabilities." At this stage, readers will gain a comprehensive understanding of zero-day vulnerabilities – those elusive and highly sought-after exploits. Experts share their insights, teaching both offensive and defensive tactics to empower readers to protect against advanced threats.

The "ZERO DAY: Novice No More" bundle is not just a compilation of books; it's a transformative learning experience. Whether you are an aspiring cybersecurity professional, a seasoned IT practitioner, or anyone concerned about the security of digital systems, this bundle will equip you with the knowledge and skills to safeguard against software vulnerabilities effectively.

Join us on this educational journey as we explore the world of software vulnerabilities, from demystifying the basics to unleashing expert-level tactics. Together, we will expose vulnerabilities and eliminate bugs, ensuring a safer and more secure digital future for all.

BOOK 1
ZERO DAY DEMYSTIFIED
A BEGINNER'S GUIDE TO UNCOVERING SOFTWARE VULNERABILITIES

ROB BOTWRIGHT

Chapter 1: Introduction to Zero Day Vulnerabilities

Zero Day vulnerabilities are a critical and complex aspect of cybersecurity, demanding a deep understanding to effectively address them. These vulnerabilities represent security flaws or weaknesses in software or hardware that are exploited by attackers before the vendor or developer has had the opportunity to release a patch or fix. The term "Zero Day" refers to the fact that, from the moment the vulnerability becomes known, there are zero days of protection for the affected system or software. This means that potential victims are at risk until a security patch or update is developed and deployed. Understanding the concept of Zero Day vulnerabilities is essential for anyone involved in cybersecurity, from novice analysts to seasoned experts. It's the first step in the journey to safeguarding systems and data from these potentially devastating threats.

The significance of Zero Day vulnerabilities in the world of cybersecurity cannot be overstated. These vulnerabilities often serve as the initial entry point for cybercriminals to infiltrate systems, launch attacks, and steal sensitive information. For this reason, they are highly sought after by malicious actors and are often sold on the black market for substantial sums. In many cases, these vulnerabilities are used in targeted attacks against high-value targets, such as government organizations, corporations, or critical infrastructure.

To gain a comprehensive understanding of Zero Day vulnerabilities, it is essential to recognize that they can exist in various types of software, including operating systems, web applications, and even firmware in embedded devices. These vulnerabilities may arise due to coding errors, design flaws, or unforeseen interactions between software components. Identifying and mitigating them requires a multi-faceted approach that encompasses vulnerability discovery, responsible disclosure, and prompt remediation.

Vulnerability analysts play a crucial role in the battle against Zero Day vulnerabilities. Their primary responsibility is to uncover these vulnerabilities before malicious actors do. This involves conducting in-depth research and analysis of software and systems, searching for weaknesses that could be exploited. Vulnerability researchers often use a combination of manual analysis and automated scanning tools to detect vulnerabilities, employing their expertise to distinguish false positives from genuine security flaws.

One of the challenges in dealing with Zero Day vulnerabilities is that they are typically undisclosed or unknown to the software vendor. This means that there are no official patches or updates available to fix the vulnerabilities when they are first discovered. Consequently, vulnerability analysts must follow responsible disclosure practices, which involve notifying the affected vendor or developer of the vulnerability and giving them a reasonable amount of time to develop and release a patch. Responsible disclosure is crucial to ensure that users are protected, but it also requires a delicate balance between protecting users and allowing vendors time to address the issue.

Advanced Exploitation Techniques Unveiled

Once Zero Day vulnerabilities are identified, they can be subject to advanced exploitation techniques by malicious actors. These techniques are designed to take advantage of the vulnerabilities for unauthorized access, data theft, or system compromise. Understanding these exploitation techniques is essential for cybersecurity professionals, as it allows them to anticipate and defend against potential threats.

Advanced exploitation techniques often involve crafting specially designed payloads or malicious code to exploit vulnerabilities in a targeted system. These payloads are carefully constructed to trigger the vulnerability and execute the attacker's code with the highest level of privilege. This can result in full system compromise or the ability to control and manipulate the compromised system.

One common type of advanced exploitation technique is known as remote code execution (RCE). In an RCE attack, an attacker exploits a vulnerability in a system or application to execute arbitrary code remotely. This can lead to a complete takeover of the target system, allowing the attacker to install malware, exfiltrate data, or carry out other malicious activities. RCE vulnerabilities are particularly dangerous and highly sought after by attackers.

Another advanced exploitation technique is privilege escalation, where an attacker exploits a vulnerability to elevate their privileges within a system. This may involve going from a regular user to an administrator or gaining access to sensitive resources that were previously off-limits. Privilege escalation can enable attackers to perform actions that would otherwise be restricted and deepen their control over a compromised system.

In addition to RCE and privilege escalation, attackers may employ techniques such as shellcode injection, buffer overflow exploits, or memory corruption attacks. These methods can be highly sophisticated and require a deep understanding of the target system's architecture and the specific vulnerability being exploited.

Ethical hackers and security professionals often study these advanced exploitation techniques to better defend against them. By understanding how attackers operate, security experts can implement preventive measures, such as intrusion detection systems, firewalls, and security patches, to mitigate the risks associated with Zero Day vulnerabilities. Additionally, security training and awareness programs help organizations and individuals stay vigilant against potential threats.

Expert Strategies for Zero Day Discovery and Research

Zero Day vulnerabilities are not only challenging for attackers to discover but also for security professionals to uncover and understand fully. Expert strategies for Zero Day discovery and research are essential to stay ahead of potential threats and vulnerabilities.

One critical aspect of Zero Day discovery is proactive research and monitoring of software and systems.

Vulnerability analysts and security researchers often engage in ongoing efforts to study and analyze software, seeking out potential weaknesses. This involves examining code, reverse engineering binaries, and conducting penetration testing to identify vulnerabilities before they are exploited by malicious actors.

Expert-level vulnerability research also involves staying up-to-date with the latest developments in the field of cybersecurity. This includes tracking security bulletins, attending conferences, and collaborating with other researchers. The rapidly evolving nature of technology means that new vulnerabilities are continually emerging, so constant vigilance is crucial.

Furthermore, expert vulnerability researchers often work with software vendors and developers to foster collaboration in identifying and addressing vulnerabilities. Establishing responsible disclosure channels and building relationships with industry stakeholders can lead to faster and more effective vulnerability mitigation.

Cutting-Edge Vulnerability Assessment Tools

In the quest to uncover and mitigate Zero Day vulnerabilities, advanced vulnerability assessment tools play a pivotal role. These tools are designed to assist security professionals in identifying and analyzing vulnerabilities within software and systems. They provide valuable insights and automation that can significantly expedite the discovery process.

Cutting-edge vulnerability assessment tools come in various forms, including both commercial and open-source solutions. These tools are equipped with sophisticated scanning engines that can analyze code, configurations, and network traffic to detect potential vulnerabilities. They utilize a combination of techniques, such as static analysis, dynamic analysis, and black-box testing, to comprehensively assess software and systems for weaknesses.

Static analysis tools examine the source code or binary of an application without executing it. They analyze the code structure, variable types, and function calls to identify potential vulnerabilities. Static analysis can be particularly effective in detecting issues like buffer overflows or insecure coding practices.

Dynamic analysis tools, on the other hand, test an application while it is running. They monitor its behavior, inputs, and interactions with the system to identify vulnerabilities that may only manifest during runtime. Dynamic analysis can uncover issues like input validation errors or memory leaks.

Black-box testing tools simulate attacks on a system without any knowledge of its internal workings. They attempt to exploit vulnerabilities from an outsider's perspective, mimicking the actions of a potential attacker. Black-box testing is valuable for evaluating the security posture of a system from an external threat perspective.

In addition to these techniques, cutting-edge vulnerability assessment tools often incorporate features like vulnerability scanning, web application testing, and database assessment. They generate detailed reports that highlight potential vulnerabilities, their severity, and recommended remediation steps.

Security professionals leverage these tools to streamline their vulnerability discovery efforts and prioritize the most critical issues. However, it's essential to remember that while these tools are powerful, they are not infallible, and human expertise remains crucial in distinguishing between false positives and genuine vulnerabilities.

Exploiting Zero Day Vulnerabilities Ethically

The existence of Zero Day vulnerabilities poses an ethical dilemma for security professionals and researchers. While these vulnerabilities must be uncovered to protect systems and data, exploiting them for personal gain or harm is unethical and often illegal. Ethical considerations are paramount when dealing with Zero Day vulnerabilities.

Ethical hackers, also known as white-hat hackers or security researchers, play a vital role in responsibly disclosing and mitigating Zero Day vulnerabilities. They use their skills and expertise to identify and report vulnerabilities to the affected vendors or developers, allowing them to develop patches and protect users. Ethical hackers act as a crucial counterbalance to malicious actors who seek to exploit these vulnerabilities for harmful purposes.

Responsible disclosure is a key ethical practice in the cybersecurity community. It involves notifying the vendor or developer of a vulnerability in a responsible and coordinated manner. This typically includes providing details of the vulnerability, proof of concept, and a reasonable timeline for the vendor to develop and release a patch. Responsible disclosure balances the need to protect users with the necessity of giving vendors adequate time to address the issue.

Ethical hackers also adhere to strict codes of conduct, ensuring that their actions are legal and ethical. They seek explicit permission before testing systems, respect confidentiality agreements, and avoid causing harm or disruption while conducting security assessments. Ethical hacking is guided by principles of integrity, transparency, and the greater good of securing digital infrastructure.

Organizations and individuals can benefit from ethical hackers by engaging them in penetration testing, vulnerability assessments, and security audits. Ethical hackers help identify and rectify vulnerabilities before malicious actors can exploit them, reducing the risk of security breaches.

In summary, Zero Day vulnerabilities represent a significant challenge in the realm of cybersecurity. Understanding the definition and significance of Zero Day vulnerabilities is the first step toward addressing them effectively. Advanced exploitation techniques, responsible discovery and disclosure, cutting-edge vulnerability assessment tools, and ethical considerations all play crucial roles in dealing with these vulnerabilities. Security professionals and ethical hackers alike must work together to protect systems, data, and individuals from the threats posed by Zero Day vulnerabilities.

Understanding the historical significance of Zero Day vulnerabilities provides valuable insights into the evolution of cybersecurity threats and the challenges they present. Throughout the history of computing and software development, vulnerabilities have always existed, but the term "Zero Day" itself is relatively modern. The concept of Zero Day vulnerabilities can be traced back to the early days of computing when the Internet was in its infancy. As computer systems and networks began to interconnect, the potential for security vulnerabilities became apparent.

The term "Zero Day" refers to the fact that, from the moment a vulnerability becomes known, there are zero days of protection for the affected system or software. This means that potential victims are at risk until a security patch or update is developed and deployed. The concept gained prominence as more sophisticated and interconnected software systems emerged in the late 20th century.

The historical significance of Zero Day vulnerabilities is closely tied to the growth of the internet and the rapid development of software applications. In the early days of computing, systems were often standalone and isolated, with limited connectivity. Vulnerabilities that were discovered typically had a limited impact and could be addressed without the urgency seen today.

However, as computer networks expanded and the internet became a global phenomenon, the potential for widespread exploitation of vulnerabilities became evident. Malicious actors realized that targeting newly discovered vulnerabilities could provide them with a significant advantage. By exploiting these vulnerabilities before they could be patched, attackers could compromise systems, steal data, or launch disruptive attacks.

The rise of Zero Day attacks in the late 20th and early 21st centuries marked a turning point in cybersecurity. These attacks demonstrated the need for a proactive approach to vulnerability management and response. Organizations and software vendors had to adapt quickly to address vulnerabilities and protect their systems and users.

One of the earliest high-profile Zero Day attacks occurred in 2003 with the Slammer/Sapphire worm, which exploited a vulnerability in Microsoft SQL Server. This worm spread rapidly across the internet, causing widespread disruption. The incident highlighted the potential impact of Zero Day vulnerabilities on critical infrastructure and the global economy.

The historical significance of Zero Day vulnerabilities extends beyond individual incidents. It underscores the constant arms race between security professionals and attackers. While security experts work to identify and patch vulnerabilities, attackers continually seek out new vulnerabilities to exploit. This cat-and-mouse game has become a defining feature of cybersecurity.

In recent years, the market for Zero Day vulnerabilities has grown considerably. Cybersecurity researchers and organizations have established programs to discover and responsibly disclose Zero Day vulnerabilities to software vendors. These programs aim to promote ethical behavior and prevent the sale of Zero Day exploits on the black market.

The historical significance of Zero Day vulnerabilities also highlights the importance of responsible disclosure. When security researchers discover a Zero Day vulnerability, they face a moral and ethical dilemma. They must balance the need to protect potential victims with the responsibility to notify the affected vendor or developer.

Responsible disclosure practices have evolved over time, with security researchers and vendors collaborating to establish guidelines for reporting and patching vulnerabilities. The goal is to ensure that users are protected without unduly exposing the vulnerability to malicious actors. Responsible disclosure has become a cornerstone of modern cybersecurity.

Despite the challenges posed by Zero Day vulnerabilities, the historical perspective provides hope for the future. The cybersecurity community has made significant advancements in vulnerability detection, threat intelligence sharing, and proactive security measures. Software vendors have adopted practices to improve the speed and efficiency of patching vulnerabilities.

Furthermore, the awareness of Zero Day vulnerabilities has grown among organizations and individuals. Security training and best practices have become integral components of cybersecurity efforts. Users are more vigilant about software updates and patches, reducing the window of opportunity for attackers.

In summary, the historical significance of Zero Day vulnerabilities underscores the ever-present challenge of cybersecurity in a connected world. Understanding the evolution of these vulnerabilities and their impact on technology and society is crucial for security professionals and organizations. While the threat of Zero Day vulnerabilities persists, responsible disclosure, proactive security measures, and increased awareness are key elements in the ongoing effort to mitigate their impact and protect digital infrastructure.

Chapter 2: Understanding the Software Landscape

The Software Development Life Cycle (SDLC) is a structured framework that guides the development of software applications from inception to deployment and maintenance. It is a fundamental process that ensures software projects are planned, executed, and managed effectively. The primary goal of the SDLC is to produce high-quality software that meets or exceeds customer expectations while staying within time and budget constraints.

The SDLC consists of a series of phases, each with its unique set of activities and objectives. These phases are typically sequential, but they can be adapted and customized to suit the specific needs of a project. The first phase of the SDLC is the Requirements Gathering phase. During this phase, project stakeholders, including customers and end-users, collaborate with the development team to define the software's functional and non-functional requirements.

Once the requirements are gathered, they are documented in detail. This documentation serves as the foundation for the entire software development process, guiding developers, testers, and other team members throughout the project. Clear and well-defined requirements are essential to ensure that the final product aligns with the customer's needs.

The next phase in the SDLC is System Design. In this phase, software architects and designers create a high-level system architecture and design based on the gathered requirements. They determine the software's structure, components, modules, and data flows. The design phase lays the groundwork for the technical implementation of the software and helps ensure that it can be efficiently developed.

Once the system design is complete, developers move on to the Implementation phase. This is where the actual coding of the software takes place. Developers write code, build software components, and integrate them into a cohesive system. This phase requires careful attention to detail and adherence to coding standards and best practices.

After the software is developed, it enters the Testing phase. During this phase, software testers and quality assurance professionals thoroughly test the application to identify defects, inconsistencies, and performance issues. Testing helps ensure that the software functions as intended and meets the specified requirements. Various testing methodologies, such as unit testing, integration testing, and user acceptance testing, are employed to validate the software's correctness and reliability.

Once the software passes testing and meets the defined criteria, it progresses to the Deployment phase. In this phase, the software is deployed to a production environment or made available to end-users. Deployment involves activities such as installation, configuration, data migration, and user training. It is a critical phase as it marks the transition from development to actual use.

Following deployment, the SDLC enters the Maintenance and Support phase. During this phase, the software is actively used by customers and end-users, and ongoing maintenance and support are provided. Maintenance activities may include bug fixes, updates, enhancements, and addressing evolving user needs. Effective maintenance ensures the long-term viability and relevance of the software.

The SDLC phases described here follow a traditional waterfall model, where each phase is completed before the next one begins. However, many modern software development approaches, such as Agile and DevOps, emphasize iterative and collaborative methodologies. These approaches promote continuous improvement, flexibility, and responsiveness to changing requirements.

Agile methodologies, for example, involve short development cycles known as "sprints," where small portions of functionality are developed, tested, and deployed incrementally. This iterative approach allows for frequent feedback from stakeholders, ensuring that the software aligns with evolving requirements.

DevOps, on the other hand, focuses on the seamless integration of development and operations teams to streamline the deployment and maintenance of software. DevOps practices emphasize automation, collaboration, and continuous delivery to achieve faster and more reliable software releases.

It's important to note that the choice of SDLC model or methodology depends on the specific project, organizational culture, and project goals. Some projects may benefit from a traditional waterfall approach, while others may thrive under an Agile or DevOps framework. In summary, the Software Development Life Cycle is a foundational process that guides the development of software applications from inception to deployment and maintenance. It encompasses phases such as Requirements Gathering, System Design, Implementation, Testing, Deployment, and Maintenance. While traditional waterfall models exist, modern approaches like Agile and DevOps promote flexibility, collaboration, and iterative development to meet evolving customer needs efficiently. Understanding and selecting the right SDLC model or methodology is crucial for successful software development projects.

Navigating the vast and complex software ecosystem can be both exciting and challenging for individuals and organizations alike. In today's interconnected world, software plays a pivotal role in almost every aspect of our lives, from mobile applications that help us stay organized to complex enterprise systems that power businesses and industries. Understanding the software ecosystem is essential for making informed decisions about software selection, integration, and management.

At the heart of the software ecosystem are software applications, also known as software programs or simply "apps." These are the tools we use to perform specific tasks or functions on our computers, smartphones, and other digital devices. Whether it's a word processing application, a photo editing tool, or a video conferencing platform, software applications are the building blocks of our digital experiences.

Beyond individual applications, the software ecosystem encompasses a wide range of categories and domains. Operating systems, such as Windows, macOS, and Linux, provide the foundational software layer that enables hardware and software to interact. These operating systems dictate how our devices function, manage resources, and execute commands.

In the realm of mobile devices, we encounter mobile operating systems like iOS and Android, which power our smartphones and tablets. Mobile apps, available through app stores, extend the functionality of these devices, offering everything from social networking to gaming.

The web browser is another crucial component of the software ecosystem. Browsers like Google Chrome, Mozilla Firefox, and Microsoft Edge allow us to access and interact with websites and web applications. The web itself represents a vast and dynamic ecosystem, where websites, web services, and cloud-based applications thrive.

Enterprise software solutions are a significant part of the ecosystem, catering to the needs of businesses and organizations. Customer relationship management (CRM) software, enterprise resource planning (ERP) systems, and collaboration tools enable businesses to streamline operations, manage data, and communicate effectively.

Open-source software is a distinctive and influential part of the software ecosystem. Open-source projects, like the Linux operating system and the Apache web server, offer software with source code that is openly available for inspection, modification, and distribution. These projects foster collaboration, innovation, and a sense of community among developers and users.

Cloud computing has reshaped the software landscape by providing scalable and on-demand access to computing resources and services. Cloud providers like Amazon Web Services (AWS), Microsoft Azure, and Google Cloud offer a wide array of tools and platforms that enable businesses to deploy and manage applications in the cloud.

In the realm of software development, programming languages are essential building blocks. Languages like Python, Java, JavaScript, and C++ empower developers to create a wide range of software applications, from web and mobile apps to artificial intelligence and machine learning solutions.

Software development frameworks and libraries further accelerate the development process. These pre-built components and tools provide developers with the means to create software more efficiently, leveraging existing code and resources.

For individuals and organizations, navigating the software ecosystem requires careful consideration of various factors. One of the most critical considerations is software selection. When choosing software applications or tools, it's essential to align them with specific needs, objectives, and preferences. Factors like user interface, functionality, scalability, and compatibility should be evaluated to ensure that the chosen software meets the desired requirements.

Integration is another significant aspect of navigating the software ecosystem. In many cases, software applications need to work seamlessly together to provide a unified user experience or to share data and functionality. Integration may involve the use of application programming interfaces (APIs), middleware, or specialized integration platforms to connect disparate software components.

Software management is an ongoing task that involves maintaining, updating, and optimizing software applications and systems. Regular updates and patches are essential to address security vulnerabilities and enhance software performance. Effective software management also includes license compliance, cost optimization, and monitoring for potential issues.

Security is a paramount concern within the software ecosystem. With the increasing prevalence of cyber threats and data breaches, safeguarding software and data is of utmost importance. This involves implementing security measures, such as encryption, access controls, and regular security audits, to protect against potential threats.

User education and training are vital components of software management. Users need to be familiar with software applications to use them effectively and securely. Training programs and user documentation can help individuals and organizations maximize the benefits of the software they employ.

The software ecosystem is continually evolving, with new technologies, trends, and innovations emerging regularly. Staying informed and adaptable is crucial for individuals and organizations navigating this dynamic landscape. Keeping up with industry news, attending conferences, and participating in user communities are ways to stay connected and informed.

In summary, the software ecosystem is a multifaceted and ever-expanding domain that encompasses a wide range of software applications, technologies, and platforms. Navigating this ecosystem involves thoughtful software selection, integration, management, and security considerations. Whether you are an individual seeking to enhance your digital experience or an organization aiming to optimize its software infrastructure, understanding the software ecosystem is a valuable endeavor.

Chapter 3: Common Types of Software Vulnerabilities

In the world of cybersecurity and software vulnerabilities, buffer overflows and stack smashing are terms that hold significant importance. These terms refer to types of software vulnerabilities and exploitation techniques that have been a focal point in the battle between security professionals and malicious actors. To understand buffer overflows and stack smashing, it's essential to delve into their definitions, how they occur, and the consequences they can have on computer systems and software applications. A buffer overflow occurs when a program writes data to a buffer or memory location outside the intended boundary, causing it to overflow into adjacent memory regions. This overflow can overwrite critical data, such as control data or return addresses, leading to unintended consequences that can be exploited by attackers. Stack smashing, on the other hand, is a specific type of buffer overflow that targets the call stack, a critical component of program execution. In stack smashing attacks, attackers manipulate the stack's contents to gain control over program execution and inject malicious code. The call stack is a data structure used by programs to keep track of function calls and their respective return addresses. It operates like a stack of function calls, with each function call pushing its return address onto the stack and popping it off when the function returns. When a buffer overflow occurs in a program, it can corrupt the call stack by overwriting return addresses or other critical data. This corruption can allow attackers to redirect the program's execution to their malicious code, effectively taking control of the program. Stack smashing attacks can have devastating consequences, as attackers can use them to execute arbitrary code with the privileges of the compromised program, potentially gaining unauthorized access to a system. To mitigate the risk of buffer overflows and stack smashing attacks, it is essential for developers to follow secure coding practices. This includes bounds checking, where developers ensure that data written to buffers does not exceed their predefined boundaries. Additionally, input validation should be performed to prevent malicious input from reaching vulnerable code segments. Using safer programming languages that include built-in memory safety features, such as bounds checking, can also help prevent buffer overflows. Address Space Layout Randomization (ASLR) is another mitigation technique that randomizes the memory addresses of key program components, making it harder for attackers to predict memory locations accurately. Similarly, Data Execution Prevention (DEP) prevents the execution of code in specific memory regions, reducing the likelihood of successful exploitation. Software developers should be aware of these techniques and incorporate them into their coding practices to minimize the risk of buffer overflows and stack smashing vulnerabilities. However, despite the best efforts of developers and security measures, buffer overflows and stack smashing vulnerabilities can still exist in software. For this reason, it is crucial to have intrusion detection and prevention systems in place to monitor and defend against potential attacks. Intrusion detection systems can identify suspicious activities that may indicate a buffer overflow or stack smashing attempt. They can raise alerts or take preventive actions to mitigate the risk. Furthermore, timely patching and updates are essential to address known vulnerabilities that could be exploited by attackers. Developers and security professionals should stay informed about security patches and apply them promptly to prevent exploitation. In the event of a buffer overflow or stack smashing vulnerability being discovered, responsible disclosure to the software vendor is essential. This allows the vendor to develop and release patches to address the vulnerability and protect users. Vendors, in turn, should respond quickly to such reports and issue patches to mitigate the risk. The battle against buffer overflows and stack smashing vulnerabilities is ongoing, and security professionals continually work to identify and address these issues. It is essential for software developers, vendors, and end-users to collaborate in this effort by following secure coding practices, implementing security measures, and promptly applying patches. Education and awareness about these vulnerabilities and their potential consequences are crucial for maintaining the security of computer systems and software applications. In summary, buffer overflows and stack smashing are significant vulnerabilities in the world of cybersecurity. They can lead to unauthorized code execution, compromising the security and integrity of computer systems. Mitigating the risk of these vulnerabilities requires a multi-faceted approach, including secure coding practices, intrusion detection systems, responsible disclosure, and timely patching. By understanding these vulnerabilities and taking proactive measures, we can enhance the security of software and protect against potential exploitation.

In the world of cybersecurity, two prevalent threats that web developers and security professionals often encounter are SQL injection and Cross-Site Scripting (XSS). These threats target web applications and can have severe consequences if not properly mitigated. SQL injection is a type of attack that occurs when malicious actors exploit vulnerabilities in an application's code to manipulate a database through SQL queries. To understand SQL injection, it's important to first grasp the role of SQL (Structured Query Language) in database operations. SQL is a language used to manage and manipulate data in relational databases, making it a fundamental component of many web applications. Web applications typically use SQL to interact with databases to retrieve, update, or delete information. SQL queries are constructed in a way that allows for precise data retrieval and management. However, when user input is not properly validated or sanitized, it can be exploited by attackers to execute arbitrary SQL commands. SQL injection attacks typically involve injecting malicious SQL code into user inputs, such as login forms or search boxes. When these inputs are not adequately validated, the malicious SQL code becomes part of the application's queries, allowing attackers to access, modify, or delete data in the database. The consequences of a successful SQL injection attack can be severe, ranging from unauthorized access to sensitive information, such as user credentials or financial data, to the complete compromise of a web application's database. Preventing SQL injection requires implementing proper input validation and sanitization techniques. Web developers should validate user inputs to ensure they conform to expected formats and do not contain malicious code. Additionally, using parameterized queries or prepared statements in code can help protect against SQL injection by separating user input from SQL commands. Cross-Site Scripting, or XSS, is another widespread web application vulnerability that attackers often exploit. XSS attacks occur when malicious scripts are injected into web pages viewed by other users. These scripts are executed within the context of the victim's browser, allowing attackers to steal session cookies, login credentials, or other sensitive information. XSS attacks are particularly dangerous because they can lead to the compromise of user accounts or the spreading of malware to unsuspecting visitors. XSS attacks can take multiple forms, including stored XSS, reflected XSS, and DOM-based XSS. Stored XSS involves injecting malicious scripts that are permanently stored on a website, making them accessible to all users who visit the affected page. Reflected XSS, on the other hand, involves injecting malicious scripts that are reflected off a web server and executed in the victim's browser when they visit a particular URL. DOM-based XSS attacks manipulate the Document Object Model (DOM) of a web page, allowing attackers to modify its structure and behavior dynamically. Preventing XSS attacks requires input validation and output encoding. Web developers should ensure that user inputs are properly validated, and any data that is displayed on a web page is correctly encoded or sanitized. Additionally, implementing security mechanisms like Content Security Policy (CSP) can help mitigate the risk of XSS attacks by specifying which resources and scripts are allowed to execute. Regularly patching and updating web application frameworks, libraries, and plugins is also crucial to address known vulnerabilities that can be exploited in XSS attacks. Both SQL injection and XSS attacks are well-documented and have been responsible for numerous data breaches and security incidents. Security professionals continuously work to discover and mitigate these vulnerabilities, and it is essential for web developers and application owners to stay informed about emerging threats and best practices for securing their applications. Web security scanners and penetration testing can also be valuable tools for identifying and addressing vulnerabilities in web applications. In summary, SQL injection and Cross-Site Scripting (XSS) are prevalent web application vulnerabilities that pose significant risks to data security and user privacy. Understanding these threats and implementing effective security measures, such as input validation, output encoding, and regular patching, is crucial for safeguarding web applications and protecting users from potential exploitation. By remaining vigilant and proactive, web developers and security professionals can significantly reduce the likelihood of successful SQL injection and XSS attacks, ultimately enhancing the overall security of web applications and the data they handle.

Chapter 4: The Role of Zero Day Exploits

Exploring the intricate world of Zero Day exploits provides a glimpse into the realm of advanced cybersecurity threats and the vulnerabilities they target. Zero Day exploits are a class of attacks that specifically target vulnerabilities in software applications or operating systems that are unknown to the software vendor. These vulnerabilities are referred to as "Zero Day" because there are zero days of protection available to users when the exploit is first discovered. In other words, no security patches or updates exist to defend against these attacks, making them particularly dangerous. The anatomy of a Zero Day exploit encompasses various elements that work in concert to compromise a target system. At its core, a Zero Day exploit consists of the following key components: the vulnerability, the exploit code, the payload, and the delivery mechanism. The vulnerability is the fundamental weakness or flaw in the software that the attacker exploits. This vulnerability can be a programming error, a design flaw, or an unintended behavior that allows an attacker to gain unauthorized access or control over the system. Identifying these vulnerabilities often requires advanced reverse engineering and security research skills. Once a vulnerability is identified, the attacker develops exploit code that takes advantage of the vulnerability to execute arbitrary commands or code on the target system. This code is specifically crafted to trigger the vulnerability and gain a foothold on the target system. The payload is the malicious code or instructions that the attacker wants to run on the compromised system. The payload can range from simple commands for data theft to more complex operations like establishing a persistent backdoor for remote control. The delivery mechanism is the method used to deliver the exploit code to the target system. This can include email attachments, malicious websites, network attacks, or even physical access to the target device. Understanding the anatomy of a Zero Day exploit is crucial for both security professionals and software vendors. For security professionals, it is essential to be aware of the potential threats posed by Zero Day exploits and to implement proactive security measures to mitigate the risk. These measures can include intrusion detection systems, network monitoring, and security awareness training for end-users. For software vendors, recognizing the presence of a vulnerability in their products and addressing it before it is exploited is of utmost importance. This involves conducting rigorous security testing, code reviews, and vulnerability assessments during the software development lifecycle. While the anatomy of a Zero Day exploit may seem straightforward, the process of discovering and exploiting Zero Day vulnerabilities is highly complex and typically conducted by skilled hackers and security researchers. The journey begins with vulnerability discovery, a process that involves identifying potential vulnerabilities in software through code analysis, fuzz testing, or other means. Once a vulnerability is identified, the attacker must develop exploit code that can trigger the vulnerability and execute the desired actions on the target system. This code often requires a deep understanding of the underlying software, its architecture, and the specific nature of the vulnerability. The payload, which contains the malicious instructions or code that the attacker wants to run on the target system, is carefully crafted to achieve the attacker's goals. Payloads can vary widely in complexity, from simple commands to complex malware. The final step in the process is the delivery mechanism, which determines how the exploit code will be delivered to the target system. Attackers may use social engineering tactics to trick users into clicking on malicious links or opening infected email attachments. Alternatively, they may employ network attacks to directly exploit vulnerabilities in the target system. One of the most significant challenges in dealing with Zero Day exploits is the lack of available defenses when the vulnerability is first discovered and exploited. Traditional security mechanisms, such as antivirus software and intrusion detection systems, often struggle to detect and block Zero Day exploits because they are based on known patterns and signatures. As a result, Zero Day exploits can remain undetected until they are actively exploited, leading to potential data breaches, system compromises, and security incidents. To address the threat of Zero Day exploits, organizations must adopt a proactive and multi-layered security approach. This includes keeping software and systems up to date with the latest security patches, employing network segmentation to limit the impact of potential breaches, and conducting regular security assessments and penetration testing to identify vulnerabilities. Additionally, user education and awareness are crucial in preventing social engineering attacks that often serve as the delivery mechanism for Zero Day exploits. While the anatomy of a Zero Day exploit may appear daunting, it is essential to recognize that proactive security measures, prompt vulnerability patching, and a well-informed and vigilant user base can significantly reduce the risk associated with these advanced threats. By staying ahead of potential attackers and prioritizing security, organizations can better protect their systems and data from the ever-evolving landscape of Zero Day exploits. In summary, understanding the anatomy of a Zero Day exploit provides valuable insights into the sophisticated world of cybersecurity threats. Zero Day exploits target vulnerabilities that are unknown to software vendors, making them particularly challenging to defend against. The process of discovering and exploiting Zero Day vulnerabilities involves intricate steps, from vulnerability discovery to the development of exploit code and payload creation. The delivery mechanism is the final piece of the puzzle, determining how the exploit code reaches the target system. Dealing with Zero Day exploits requires a proactive and multi-layered security approach, including patch management, network segmentation, and user education. By staying vigilant and prepared, organizations can better defend against these advanced threats and protect their systems and data.

Exploring the real-world implications of Zero Day exploits sheds light on the tangible consequences that these advanced cybersecurity threats can have. Zero Day exploits pose significant risks to individuals, organizations, and even nations, making them a focal point in the ongoing battle against cyber threats. One of the most immediate and concerning implications of Zero Day exploits is the potential for data breaches. When attackers successfully exploit a Zero Day vulnerability, they can gain unauthorized access to sensitive data, including personal information, financial records, and intellectual property. This breach of privacy can have severe consequences, leading to identity theft, financial losses, and reputational damage for individuals and organizations alike. Moreover, Zero Day exploits can be leveraged for espionage purposes. State-sponsored actors and cybercriminal groups may exploit Zero Days to infiltrate government agencies, corporations, or critical infrastructure systems. Once inside, they can gather intelligence, monitor communications, or disrupt operations, compromising national security and economic stability. Another real-world implication of Zero Day exploits is the potential for widespread malware outbreaks. Attackers can use Zero Days to deliver malware payloads to a large number of systems. These malware infections can lead to system compromises, data theft, and the creation of botnets, which can be used for various malicious purposes, including launching distributed denial-of-service (DDoS) attacks or spreading further malware. Furthermore, the financial impact of Zero Day exploits should not be underestimated. The cost of responding to a Zero Day attack can be substantial, including expenses related to incident response, legal liabilities, and regulatory fines. Organizations may also face financial losses due to stolen intellectual property, disrupted business operations, or reputational damage, which can erode customer trust and investor confidence. In the realm of critical infrastructure, the consequences of Zero Day exploits can be catastrophic. Zero Days targeting industrial control systems (ICS) or supervisory control and data acquisition (SCADA) systems can result in physical damage or disruption of essential services. For example, an attack on a power grid's control system could lead to widespread power outages, affecting homes, businesses, and public safety. The healthcare sector is not immune to the real-world implications of Zero Day exploits. Attacks on healthcare organizations can compromise patient data, disrupt medical services, and even endanger lives. For instance, a Zero Day attack on a hospital's electronic health record (EHR) system could lead to incorrect patient information, delayed treatments, or incorrect medication dosages. Furthermore, the proliferation of Internet of Things (IoT) devices has introduced new vulnerabilities that can be exploited through Zero Day attacks. These devices, from smart thermostats to connected vehicles, often lack robust security measures, making them susceptible to exploitation. Zero Day exploits targeting IoT devices can lead to unauthorized access, data breaches, and even physical safety risks. The implications of Zero Day exploits extend beyond immediate financial and operational consequences. They can also erode trust in technology and the digital economy. When individuals and organizations become victims of Zero Day attacks, they may lose confidence in the security of online services and hesitate to embrace new technologies. This can hinder digital innovation and slow down the adoption of emerging technologies, limiting their potential benefits. Additionally, the emergence of a thriving market for Zero Day vulnerabilities and exploits has raised ethical questions. While security researchers and organizations may seek to responsibly disclose and patch vulnerabilities, there is also a lucrative underground market for Zero Days. Malicious actors may buy and sell Zero Day exploits to further their criminal activities, creating a moral dilemma for those involved in the cybersecurity community. To address the real-world implications of Zero Day exploits, a multi-faceted approach is required. Vigilant threat intelligence and monitoring can help organizations detect and respond to Zero Day threats promptly. Implementing robust security measures, such as network segmentation, intrusion detection systems, and security patches, is crucial for mitigating the risk. Furthermore, international cooperation and information sharing among governments, organizations, and security researchers can enhance the collective defense against Zero Day threats. Responsible disclosure practices, where security researchers report Zero Day vulnerabilities to vendors, are essential for facilitating timely patches and protecting users. Education and cybersecurity awareness initiatives can empower individuals and organizations to recognize and defend against Zero Day threats effectively. In summary, the real-world implications of Zero Day exploits are far-reaching and can have devastating consequences for individuals, organizations, and society as a whole. These consequences encompass data breaches, espionage, malware outbreaks, financial losses, critical infrastructure disruptions, and erosion of trust in technology. Addressing the challenges posed by Zero Day exploits requires a comprehensive and collaborative approach that combines threat intelligence, robust security measures, responsible disclosure, and cybersecurity education. By working together, we can strengthen our defenses against Zero Day threats and minimize their impact on the digital world.

Chapter 5: Identifying Vulnerabilities in Code

Leveraging static code analysis techniques is a fundamental aspect of ensuring the security and quality of software applications. Static code analysis involves the examination of source code without its execution, enabling developers and security professionals to identify potential issues and vulnerabilities. This proactive approach to code analysis helps catch problems early in the development process, reducing the cost and complexity of fixing them later. One of the primary goals of static code analysis is to identify security vulnerabilities that can be exploited by malicious actors. These vulnerabilities may include issues like SQL injection, Cross-Site Scripting (XSS), and buffer overflows, which can lead to data breaches and other security incidents. Static analysis tools can scan source code for patterns and coding practices that are indicative of these vulnerabilities, helping developers discover and remediate them. Another critical aspect of static code analysis is the identification of coding errors and software defects that can impact the reliability and functionality of an application. These errors may lead to crashes, incorrect results, or unexpected behavior in the software. By detecting and addressing such issues early in the development cycle, static analysis helps improve the overall quality and stability of the application. Static code analysis tools employ a variety of techniques to analyze source code. One common approach is the use of pattern matching, where the tool searches for predefined patterns or signatures that indicate potential vulnerabilities or issues. For example, a static analysis tool might search for SQL queries constructed using user inputs without proper validation, which could suggest a SQL injection vulnerability. Another technique used in static code analysis is data flow analysis. This involves tracing the flow of data through the code to identify potential security or logic flaws. Data flow analysis can help pinpoint issues like information leakage, where sensitive data is unintentionally exposed. Control flow analysis is another technique employed by static analysis tools. It examines how program control flows through the code, looking for anomalies or potential security vulnerabilities. For instance, control flow analysis can identify situations where untrusted input directly influences program execution, indicating a potential security weakness. Moreover, static code analysis tools often incorporate knowledge about common programming pitfalls and security best practices. They use this knowledge to provide developers with actionable insights and recommendations for improving the code. These recommendations can include suggesting code changes, highlighting potential issues, or providing explanations and references to relevant security guidelines. Static code analysis can be integrated into the software development lifecycle at various stages. Many organizations incorporate it into their continuous integration and continuous delivery (CI/CD) pipelines, where code is automatically analyzed as part of the build and deployment process. This allows for quick feedback to developers, helping them catch and fix issues before code is promoted to production. Static analysis tools are available for various programming languages and development environments. They range from open-source options to commercial solutions, each with its own set of features and capabilities. When choosing a static analysis tool, organizations should consider factors such as language support, integration options, reporting capabilities, and the tool's ability to detect specific vulnerabilities relevant to their applications. While static code analysis offers numerous benefits, it is not a silver bullet and has its limitations. One limitation is the potential for false positives and false negatives. False positives occur when the tool identifies issues that are not actual vulnerabilities, leading to wasted time and effort in reviewing and addressing them. False negatives, on the other hand, occur when the tool misses real vulnerabilities, potentially leaving the application exposed to security risks. To minimize these limitations, it's essential to configure and fine-tune static analysis tools to the specific needs of the application and organization. Additionally, static code analysis is most effective when used in conjunction with other security practices, such as dynamic application security testing (DAST), penetration testing, and code reviews. These complementary approaches help provide a comprehensive assessment of an application's security posture. Incorporating static code analysis into an organization's software development process requires not only the use of the right tools but also a commitment to fostering a security-aware culture. Developers should receive training on secure coding practices and be encouraged to prioritize security throughout the development lifecycle. Furthermore, collaboration between development and security teams is crucial to ensure that identified issues are addressed promptly and that security remains a shared responsibility. In summary, leveraging static code analysis techniques is a vital step in enhancing the security and quality of software applications. Static analysis tools help identify security vulnerabilities, coding errors, and defects early in the development process, reducing the risk of costly issues in production. These tools employ various techniques, such as pattern matching, data flow analysis, and control flow analysis, to analyze source code and provide actionable insights to developers. While static code analysis has its limitations, it plays a valuable role in a comprehensive application security strategy when used in conjunction with other security practices. Ultimately, embracing static code analysis requires a commitment to security awareness, training, and collaboration, fostering a culture where software security is a top priority.

Dynamic code analysis and testing strategies play a crucial role in ensuring the security and reliability of software applications. Unlike static code analysis, which examines source code without execution, dynamic analysis involves running the software and analyzing its behavior in real-time. Dynamic analysis provides valuable insights into how an application behaves when executed, helping to identify runtime issues, security vulnerabilities, and performance bottlenecks. One of the primary objectives of dynamic code analysis is to detect vulnerabilities and weaknesses that may not be apparent from static analysis alone. While static analysis focuses on potential code-level issues, dynamic analysis assesses how an application interacts with its environment and handles various inputs and scenarios during runtime. This includes detecting vulnerabilities such as injection attacks, authentication bypasses, and access control flaws that may only manifest when the software is running. Dynamic analysis tools, commonly known as dynamic application security testing (DAST) tools, interact with the running application, sending different inputs and payloads to identify security weaknesses. For example, a DAST tool may attempt SQL injection by sending malicious input to a web application's input fields to see if it can manipulate the database. Another important aspect of dynamic analysis is the detection of runtime errors and exceptions. These errors can lead to application crashes, data corruption, or unpredictable behavior. Dynamic analysis tools monitor the application's execution, capturing errors and exceptions as they occur, which can be instrumental in diagnosing and fixing issues. Performance profiling is another area where dynamic analysis excels. It helps developers identify bottlenecks and areas of code that can be optimized to improve an application's performance. By analyzing memory usage, CPU utilization, and other metrics during runtime, dynamic analysis tools provide valuable insights into areas that may require optimization. Dynamic analysis also allows for the assessment of security controls and mitigations during runtime. It can help verify if security mechanisms like access controls, authentication, and authorization are effectively enforced when the application is in operation. By simulating real-world attack scenarios, dynamic analysis tools can identify potential weaknesses and misconfigurations that might be exploited by malicious actors. While dynamic analysis provides many benefits, it also has its challenges and limitations. One limitation is that dynamic analysis tools are typically less effective at finding certain types of vulnerabilities compared to static analysis. For instance, they may struggle to identify issues related to code quality, data leakage, and authentication issues that require specific test scenarios. Moreover, dynamic analysis requires the application to be in a running state, which can make it challenging to test certain components or configurations. Additionally, dynamic analysis may produce false positives and false negatives, requiring human interpretation and validation of results. To address these limitations and maximize the benefits of dynamic analysis, organizations should integrate it into their software development lifecycle. DAST tools can be used during development, testing, and even in production environments to continuously assess the security and performance of applications. Moreover, dynamic analysis should be part of a broader application security strategy that includes static analysis, penetration testing, and secure coding practices.

Collaboration between development and security teams is essential to ensure that identified issues are addressed promptly and that security remains a shared responsibility. It's also important to regularly update and maintain dynamic analysis tools to keep pace with evolving threats and technologies. Incorporating security testing into the CI/CD pipeline is another best practice. Automating dynamic analysis as part of the build and deployment process helps catch issues early, reducing the cost and complexity of fixing them later. Moreover, security testing in production environments can help identify vulnerabilities that may only manifest in real-world scenarios. In summary, dynamic code analysis and testing strategies are indispensable components of a comprehensive application security program. Dynamic analysis provides insights into runtime vulnerabilities, errors, and performance bottlenecks that may elude static analysis. While it has limitations, effective integration of dynamic analysis into the software development lifecycle can help identify and mitigate security risks and ensure the reliability and performance of applications. Collaboration, automation, and a commitment to security are key factors in harnessing the power of dynamic code analysis and testing strategies to create more secure and robust software.

Chapter 6: Vulnerability Scanning Tools for Beginners

In the world of cybersecurity, vulnerability scanning plays a pivotal role in identifying weaknesses and potential entry points for attackers in computer systems and networks. It serves as an essential proactive measure to enhance the security posture of organizations. Vulnerability scanning involves the automated process of systematically scanning and assessing computer systems, networks, and applications to discover known vulnerabilities. These vulnerabilities can range from missing security patches and misconfigurations to software flaws and weak passwords. The primary objective of vulnerability scanning is to pinpoint areas of potential risk and provide organizations with the information needed to address these vulnerabilities before they can be exploited. One of the key advantages of vulnerability scanning is its scalability and efficiency. Automated scanning tools can rapidly assess a large number of systems and applications, making it a cost-effective way to identify and prioritize security issues. Vulnerability scanning is not a new concept; it has been a fundamental practice in cybersecurity for many years. However, the importance of vulnerability scanning has grown significantly in today's digital landscape, where cyber threats continue to evolve and become more sophisticated. As technology advances and organizations rely more on digital infrastructure, the attack surface for potential vulnerabilities has expanded, making regular scanning and assessment a critical part of an organization's cybersecurity strategy. Vulnerability scanning can be categorized into two main types: network-based and application-based. Network-based vulnerability scanning focuses on identifying vulnerabilities in network infrastructure, such as routers, switches, and firewalls, as well as in the operating systems and services running on networked devices. These scans help organizations identify weaknesses that could be exploited to gain unauthorized access to network resources or disrupt network operations. On the other hand, application-based vulnerability scanning concentrates on assessing web applications, web services, and other software applications. These scans aim to uncover vulnerabilities that might be exploited to compromise the confidentiality, integrity, or availability of data processed by the application. Common vulnerabilities identified in web applications include SQL injection, Cross-Site Scripting (XSS), and security misconfigurations. The process of vulnerability scanning typically follows a well-defined workflow. It begins with the selection of the target systems or applications to be scanned. Organizations can choose to scan their entire network, specific subnets, or individual systems based on their security requirements and priorities. Once the target scope is defined, the scanning tool initiates the scanning process by sending probes or requests to the selected systems or applications. These probes are designed to interact with the target and gather information about the configuration and software running on the system. As the scanning tool interacts with the target, it compares the collected information against a database of known vulnerabilities. This database is regularly updated to include the latest security vulnerabilities and their associated details. When a vulnerability match is found during the scan, it is reported to the organization's security team or administrators. The report typically includes information about the identified vulnerability, its severity, and recommendations for remediation. Severity ratings help organizations prioritize which vulnerabilities to address first, focusing on those that pose the most significant risk. Once vulnerabilities are identified, organizations can take remediation actions to address the issues. Remediation may involve applying security patches, reconfiguring settings, updating software, or implementing other security measures to mitigate the risk. It's important to note that vulnerability scanning is not a one-time activity but an ongoing process. The digital landscape is constantly evolving, and new vulnerabilities emerge regularly. Therefore, organizations should establish a routine scanning schedule to ensure that their systems and applications remain secure over time. Additionally, vulnerability scanning can be complemented by penetration testing, which involves simulating cyberattacks to assess the effectiveness of security defenses. Penetration testing helps organizations understand how attackers might exploit vulnerabilities and provides valuable insights into potential weaknesses in their security posture. In summary, vulnerability scanning is a critical component of modern cybersecurity practices. It helps organizations identify and mitigate security vulnerabilities before they can be exploited by malicious actors. By conducting regular vulnerability scans and promptly addressing identified issues, organizations can enhance their security posture and reduce the risk of cyberattacks and data breaches.

Selecting the right scanning tools is a critical step in establishing an effective vulnerability scanning program. These tools play a crucial role in identifying and assessing vulnerabilities in your organization's computer systems, networks, and applications. Choosing the most suitable scanning tools requires careful consideration of various factors, including your organization's specific needs and objectives. One of the first factors to consider when selecting scanning tools is the scope of your scanning requirements. Are you primarily interested in network-based scanning to assess your network infrastructure, or do you need application-based scanning to evaluate your web applications and software? Understanding the scope will help you narrow down your options and focus on tools that align with your goals. Another important consideration is the types of vulnerabilities you want to target. Some scanning tools specialize in specific types of vulnerabilities, such as web application vulnerabilities or operating system weaknesses. Identifying your organization's vulnerability landscape will help you choose tools that are capable of detecting the vulnerabilities most relevant to your environment.

Scanning tools vary in terms of their deployment models, and it's essential to select tools that fit seamlessly into your existing infrastructure. Some tools are designed for on-premises deployment, allowing you to run scans within your network. Others offer cloud-based scanning solutions, which can be advantageous for organizations with distributed or hybrid environments. Consider your organization's network architecture and requirements to determine the most suitable deployment model. Compatibility with your existing systems and technologies is another critical factor to assess. Ensure that the scanning tools you choose can integrate with your current network and security infrastructure, including firewalls, intrusion detection systems, and security information and event management (SIEM) solutions. Effective integration can streamline the scanning process and enhance your ability to respond to vulnerabilities. Scanning tools vary in terms of the scanning techniques they employ, such as active or passive scanning. Active scanning involves sending probes and requests to target systems to assess their vulnerabilities actively. Passive scanning, on the other hand, observes network traffic and system behavior to identify vulnerabilities without direct interaction. Understanding the advantages and limitations of each technique will help you select the right scanning tools based on your organization's requirements. Consider the scalability of scanning tools, especially if your organization's network and application landscape is vast and continuously evolving. Ensure that the tools can handle the volume of scanning required without causing performance issues or disruptions. Scalability is crucial to maintain the efficiency and effectiveness of your vulnerability scanning program as your organization grows. Ease of use and the availability of user-friendly interfaces are essential factors to consider, particularly if you have a diverse team of users, including security professionals and IT administrators. Intuitive interfaces and reporting capabilities can simplify the scanning process and facilitate collaboration among team members. Additionally, consider the reporting and analytics features offered by scanning tools. The ability to generate comprehensive and customizable reports is essential for presenting findings to stakeholders and management. Look for tools that provide detailed vulnerability reports, including severity ratings, remediation recommendations, and historical data for trend analysis. It's also beneficial if the tools offer integration with third-party reporting and analytics solutions. Cost is a significant consideration when selecting scanning tools, as the pricing models for these tools can vary widely. Evaluate the total cost of ownership, including licensing fees, maintenance, and support costs. Consider whether the pricing model aligns with your organization's budget and long-term sustainability. Additionally, some scanning tools offer free or open-source options, which can be a cost-effective choice for smaller organizations or those with limited resources. Vendor reputation and support are critical factors in the selection process. Choose vendors with a proven track record in the cybersecurity industry and a history of regular updates and support. Vendor responsiveness to security vulnerabilities and issues is essential to ensure that your scanning tools remain effective over time. Lastly, consider the scalability of scanning tools, especially if your organization's network and application landscape is vast and continuously evolving. Ensure that the tools can handle the volume of scanning required without causing performance issues or disruptions. Scalability is crucial to maintain the efficiency and effectiveness of your vulnerability scanning program as your organization grows. In summary, selecting the right scanning tools is a strategic decision that can significantly impact your organization's ability to identify and mitigate vulnerabilities. Consider factors such as the scope of your scanning requirements, the types of vulnerabilities you want to target, deployment models, compatibility with existing systems, scanning techniques, scalability, ease of use, reporting capabilities, cost, vendor reputation, and support. By carefully evaluating these factors and aligning them with your organization's specific needs and objectives, you can choose scanning tools that enhance your cybersecurity posture and contribute to the overall security of your digital assets.

Chapter 7: Reporting and Documenting Vulnerabilities

Accurate reporting holds a pivotal role in various aspects of our lives, from journalism to business, and especially in the realm of cybersecurity. In the context of cybersecurity, accurate reporting serves as a cornerstone of effective risk management and incident response. It involves the timely and precise documentation of security-related events, vulnerabilities, incidents, and their outcomes. Accurate reporting not only helps organizations understand their current security posture but also supports informed decision-making and compliance efforts. One of the primary reasons accurate reporting is essential in cybersecurity is its role in incident detection and response. When a security incident occurs, such as a data breach or a cyberattack, accurate reporting allows organizations to gather critical information about the incident's nature, scope, and impact. This information is invaluable in determining the appropriate response measures, such as containment, eradication, and recovery. Accurate reporting also aids in the preservation of evidence, which is crucial for forensic investigations and potential legal actions. Security incidents often involve complex technical details and timelines, and without accurate reporting, important evidence may be lost or overlooked. Furthermore, accurate reporting supports regulatory compliance requirements that organizations must adhere to.

Various industries and regions have established cybersecurity regulations and standards that mandate reporting specific security events and breaches. Failure to provide accurate and timely reports can result in regulatory penalties and legal consequences for organizations. Accurate reporting helps organizations demonstrate their commitment to compliance and data protection. It provides a record of security incidents and measures taken to mitigate risks, which can be presented to regulatory authorities as evidence of due diligence. Accurate reporting also plays a vital role in risk assessment and management. By documenting security vulnerabilities, incidents, and their impacts, organizations can assess the likelihood and potential consequences of future incidents. This information enables organizations to prioritize security investments and implement preventive measures effectively. Moreover, accurate reporting facilitates communication and collaboration among different teams within an organization. In large enterprises, cybersecurity incidents and vulnerabilities often involve multiple departments, including IT, security, legal, and communications. Accurate reporting provides a common language and understanding of the situation, enabling these teams to work together seamlessly to address security challenges. Additionally, reporting helps organizations identify trends and patterns in security incidents and vulnerabilities. By analyzing historical data, organizations can gain insights into emerging threats and vulnerabilities, allowing them to proactively adapt their security strategies. Accurate reporting also aids in the assessment of security controls and the effectiveness of security measures. It allows organizations to track the performance of security technologies, such as firewalls, intrusion detection systems, and antivirus solutions. If anomalies or issues are detected through reporting, organizations can take corrective actions to improve their security posture. Furthermore, accurate reporting supports accountability and transparency in cybersecurity efforts. When security incidents occur, stakeholders, including customers, partners, and employees, expect organizations to be transparent about the situation and the actions taken. Accurate reporting helps organizations provide clear and truthful information, fostering trust and confidence in their cybersecurity practices. However, achieving accurate reporting in cybersecurity can be challenging. Security incidents can be complex, involving numerous technical details, and the accuracy of reports may depend on the skills and knowledge of the individuals responsible for documenting the events. To address this challenge, organizations should invest in training and awareness programs to ensure that staff members understand the importance of accurate reporting and possess the necessary skills. They should also implement incident response and reporting procedures that guide employees through the reporting process. Automation and incident response tools can help streamline the reporting process and reduce the risk of human error. Moreover, organizations should conduct regular reviews and audits of their reporting practices to identify areas for improvement and ensure ongoing accuracy. In summary, accurate reporting is of paramount importance in cybersecurity. It supports incident detection and response, regulatory compliance, risk assessment, communication and collaboration, trend analysis, security control assessment, and accountability. While achieving accurate reporting can be challenging, organizations can overcome these challenges through training, procedures, automation, and ongoing reviews. By prioritizing accurate reporting, organizations can strengthen their cybersecurity posture and build trust with stakeholders in an increasingly digital and interconnected world.

Documentation is a vital aspect of any organization's operations, providing a structured means of capturing and preserving knowledge, processes, and information. In the context of cybersecurity, documentation takes on an even greater significance, as it plays a crucial role in enhancing security, incident response, and compliance efforts. Effective documentation not only supports an organization's ability to defend against threats but also facilitates informed decision-making and continuous improvement. One of the fundamental best practices in documentation is to establish a clear and consistent structure. Documentation should follow a standardized format that is easily understandable and accessible to all relevant stakeholders. Consistency in structure and formatting helps ensure that information is organized and can be quickly located when needed. Moreover, it simplifies the onboarding process for new team members who can familiarize themselves with the documentation more efficiently. Documentation should be well-organized, with clear headings, subheadings, and a table of contents if necessary, to facilitate navigation. Each document should have a clear title and a version number, ensuring that users can easily identify the document's purpose and track changes. Another important aspect of documentation is the use of plain and straightforward language. While technical topics are often complex, documentation should strive for clarity and avoid unnecessary jargon. This ensures that the documentation is accessible to a broader audience, including non-technical staff and stakeholders. Furthermore, documentation should be kept up to date. Outdated or inaccurate documentation can lead to misunderstandings, mistakes, and security vulnerabilities. Organizations should establish a regular review and revision process to ensure that documentation remains current and relevant. This process may involve assigning responsibility to specific individuals or teams for updating and verifying the accuracy of documents. Documentation should also be versioned and dated to track changes and revisions effectively. A version history helps users understand when updates were made and what changes were implemented. Moreover, documentation should be stored and managed securely. Sensitive or confidential information may be included in documentation, such as security policies, procedures, and incident reports. Organizations should implement access controls and encryption to protect this information from unauthorized access or disclosure. Secure document storage ensures that sensitive data is safeguarded and compliant with data protection regulations. It is essential to consider the accessibility of documentation. Documentation should be readily available to authorized users when they need it. This can be achieved through the use of document management systems, cloud-based repositories, or well-structured network folders. Accessibility also means that documents should be searchable, allowing users to quickly find the information they require. Effective documentation should include comprehensive and detailed information. This means documenting not only what needs to be done but also how it should be done. For example, security policies should outline not only the rules but also the procedures for compliance. Additionally, documentation should cover various scenarios, including best practices, troubleshooting guides, and incident response procedures. A well-documented incident response plan, for instance, should provide step-by-step instructions for handling different types of security incidents. Documentation should also include references to external resources, such as security standards, guidelines, and relevant laws and regulations. These references provide users with additional context and resources for further research. Furthermore, documentation should support traceability. Traceability allows organizations to link different documents and pieces of information to create a comprehensive view of processes and procedures. For instance, a security policy document may reference a network diagram, which, in turn, references specific firewall rules and access control lists. This interconnectedness provides a holistic understanding of the organization's security measures. Effective documentation also incorporates documentation controls. Document controls include measures such as document approval processes, change management, and document retention policies. These controls help maintain the integrity of documentation and ensure that it remains accurate and up to date. They also provide a framework for managing changes to documentation systematically. Documentation should be designed to be flexible and adaptable. Cybersecurity is a dynamic field, and organizations must be prepared to respond to evolving threats and technologies. Documentation should not be overly rigid but instead should allow for updates and adjustments as needed. This flexibility ensures that documentation remains relevant and aligned with the organization's security needs. Moreover, documentation should support knowledge sharing and collaboration. It should encourage teams to contribute their expertise and insights to improve processes and procedures continually. Collaborative documentation platforms can facilitate teamwork and knowledge sharing among different departments and teams. Lastly, documentation should be regularly reviewed and tested. Reviewing documentation helps identify gaps, inaccuracies, and areas for improvement. Testing documentation involves simulating real-world scenarios to ensure that procedures and processes work as intended. For example, conducting tabletop exercises can help assess the effectiveness of incident response procedures documented in a cybersecurity playbook. In summary, documentation best practices are essential for organizations to enhance their cybersecurity posture and overall operational efficiency. Effective documentation involves establishing a clear and consistent structure, using plain language, keeping documents up to date, securing sensitive information, ensuring accessibility, providing comprehensive and detailed information, supporting traceability, incorporating documentation controls, allowing for flexibility, promoting collaboration, and conducting regular reviews and testing. By following these best practices, organizations can create documentation that not only serves as a valuable resource but also contributes to their resilience in the face of cybersecurity challenges.

Chapter 8: Remediation Strategies for Novices

Understanding the basics of remediation is essential for organizations striving to maintain a strong cybersecurity posture. Remediation refers to the process of identifying, addressing, and mitigating vulnerabilities, weaknesses, and security issues within an organization's IT environment. It plays a critical role in minimizing risks, protecting data, and ensuring the integrity and availability of systems and applications. One of the primary objectives of remediation is to reduce the attack surface, making it more challenging for malicious actors to exploit vulnerabilities. To achieve this, organizations need to have a clear understanding of the remediation process and its fundamental principles. Remediation typically begins with vulnerability assessment and identification. This phase involves scanning systems, networks, and applications to detect vulnerabilities and weaknesses. Vulnerability scanners, both automated and manual, are used to identify known vulnerabilities and assess the overall security posture. Once vulnerabilities are identified, they are prioritized based on severity, potential impact, and exploitability. Not all vulnerabilities pose the same level of risk, and prioritization helps organizations focus their remediation efforts on the most critical issues first. Vulnerabilities that are easily exploitable and have severe consequences often take precedence. After prioritization, organizations develop a remediation plan.

The plan outlines the specific actions and steps required to address each identified vulnerability. It includes timelines, responsible individuals or teams, and the resources needed for remediation. The remediation plan should also consider the potential impact of remediation actions on the organization's operations and prioritize actions accordingly. Remediation actions can take various forms, depending on the nature of the vulnerability. Common remediation strategies include applying security patches and updates, reconfiguring systems, strengthening access controls, and implementing security measures. Security patches are essential for addressing software vulnerabilities and ensuring that systems and applications are up to date with the latest security fixes. Timely patching is crucial, as attackers often target known vulnerabilities for exploitation. In addition to patching, organizations may need to adjust configurations to eliminate security weaknesses. This may involve modifying firewall rules, disabling unnecessary services, or strengthening password policies. Access controls play a significant role in remediation by ensuring that only authorized users can access sensitive resources. Implementing multi-factor authentication (MFA) and least privilege access principles can help enhance access controls. In some cases, remediation may involve the installation of additional security tools and measures, such as intrusion detection systems or endpoint protection solutions. Once remediation actions are executed, organizations conduct validation and testing to ensure that the vulnerabilities have been successfully addressed. This phase involves retesting systems and applications to confirm that the identified vulnerabilities have been mitigated and that the remediation actions did not introduce new issues. Validation and testing help ensure the effectiveness of remediation efforts and provide assurance that the organization is now better protected against threats. Documentation is a critical aspect of the remediation process. Organizations should maintain detailed records of all remediation activities, including the identification of vulnerabilities, the development and execution of the remediation plan, and the results of validation and testing. This documentation serves as an audit trail and provides transparency into the organization's security practices. It can be valuable for compliance purposes and in demonstrating due diligence in addressing security vulnerabilities. Continuous monitoring is an integral part of remediation. Even after vulnerabilities are addressed, organizations must remain vigilant and monitor their IT environment for any signs of new vulnerabilities or emerging threats. Regular security assessments and ongoing vulnerability scanning help ensure that the organization remains proactive in identifying and remediating security issues. Moreover, a strong incident response plan is essential as part of the remediation process. While remediation efforts aim to prevent security incidents, organizations must be prepared to respond swiftly and effectively if a breach occurs. An incident response plan outlines the steps to take when a security incident is detected, including containment, eradication, recovery, and communication. In summary, understanding the basics of remediation is crucial for organizations seeking to bolster their cybersecurity defenses. The remediation process involves vulnerability assessment and identification, prioritization, development of a remediation plan, execution of remediation actions, validation and testing, documentation, continuous monitoring, and incident response planning. By following these fundamental principles of remediation, organizations can reduce their attack surface, minimize risks, and maintain a resilient cybersecurity posture in the face of evolving threats.

In the realm of cybersecurity, having a clear understanding of step-by-step remediation approaches is vital for organizations seeking to strengthen their security posture and protect against vulnerabilities and threats. These approaches provide a systematic and structured way to identify, assess, and mitigate security issues within an organization's IT environment. By following these steps, organizations can effectively reduce their attack surface, minimize risks, and enhance their overall cybersecurity resilience. The first step in a step-by-step remediation approach is the identification of vulnerabilities and security weaknesses. This involves conducting regular vulnerability assessments and scans of systems, networks, and applications to pinpoint potential vulnerabilities. Vulnerability scanning tools are commonly used to automate this process, providing organizations with a comprehensive list of security issues. Once vulnerabilities are identified, they should be prioritized based on factors such as severity, potential impact, and exploitability. Not all vulnerabilities pose the same level of risk, and prioritization ensures that organizations focus their remediation efforts on the most critical issues. Vulnerabilities with a high severity rating and a high potential for exploitation typically take precedence. After prioritization, organizations develop a remediation plan. The remediation plan outlines the specific actions and steps required to address each identified vulnerability. It includes details such as timelines, responsible individuals or teams, and the resources needed for remediation. The plan should also consider the potential impact of remediation actions on the organization's operations and prioritize actions accordingly. Remediation actions can take various forms, depending on the nature of the vulnerability. Common remediation strategies include applying security patches and updates, reconfiguring systems, strengthening access controls, and implementing security measures. Security patches are crucial for addressing software vulnerabilities and ensuring that systems and applications are up to date with the latest security fixes. Timely patching is essential, as attackers often target known vulnerabilities for exploitation. In addition to patching, organizations may need to adjust configurations to eliminate security weaknesses. This may involve modifying firewall rules, disabling unnecessary services, or strengthening password policies. Access controls play a significant role in remediation by ensuring that only authorized users can access sensitive resources. Implementing multi-factor authentication (MFA) and following least privilege access principles can help enhance access controls. In some cases, remediation may involve the installation of additional security tools and measures, such as intrusion detection systems or endpoint protection solutions. Once remediation actions are executed, organizations conduct validation and testing to ensure that the vulnerabilities have been successfully addressed. This phase involves retesting systems and applications to confirm that the identified vulnerabilities have been mitigated and that the remediation actions did not introduce new issues. Validation and testing help ensure the effectiveness of remediation efforts and provide assurance that the organization is now better protected against threats. Documentation is a critical aspect of the remediation process. Organizations should maintain detailed records of all remediation activities, including the identification of vulnerabilities, the development and execution of the remediation plan, and the results of validation and testing. This documentation serves as an audit trail and provides transparency into the organization's security practices. It can be valuable for compliance purposes and in demonstrating due diligence in addressing security vulnerabilities. Continuous monitoring is an integral part of remediation. Even after vulnerabilities are addressed, organizations must remain vigilant and monitor their IT environment for any signs of new vulnerabilities or emerging threats. Regular security assessments and ongoing vulnerability scanning help ensure that the organization remains proactive in identifying and remediating security issues. Moreover, a robust incident response plan is essential as part of the remediation process. While remediation efforts aim to prevent security incidents, organizations must be prepared to respond swiftly and effectively if a breach occurs. An incident response plan outlines the steps to take when a security incident is detected, including containment, eradication, recovery, and communication. In summary, step-by-step remediation approaches are a critical component of an organization's cybersecurity strategy. These approaches provide a systematic and structured way to identify, assess, and mitigate vulnerabilities and security weaknesses. By following these steps, organizations can reduce their attack surface, minimize risks, and enhance their overall cybersecurity resilience in an ever-evolving threat landscape.

Chapter 9: Best Practices in Software Security

Understanding software security fundamentals is essential in today's digital landscape, where the reliance on software applications is pervasive, and the potential for security vulnerabilities is ever-present. Software security encompasses a set of principles, practices, and techniques designed to protect software applications from threats, vulnerabilities, and attacks. By grasping these fundamentals, individuals and organizations can build a solid foundation for ensuring the security and integrity of their software systems. At the core of software security is the concept of threat modeling, which involves identifying and evaluating potential threats and vulnerabilities that could affect a software application. This process begins with a comprehensive analysis of the application's architecture, design, and functionality. Threat modeling helps stakeholders understand the potential risks and security weaknesses that need to be addressed during development and maintenance. One of the fundamental principles of software security is the principle of least privilege, which emphasizes limiting access and permissions to the minimum necessary for users or components to perform their functions. By adhering to this principle, software developers can reduce the attack surface, making it more challenging for malicious actors to exploit vulnerabilities. Another essential concept in software security is input validation. Applications often accept input from users, whether through web forms, command-line arguments, or other means. Input validation involves thoroughly examining and validating user input to ensure it meets specific criteria and does not contain malicious or unexpected data. Failure to validate input properly can lead to security vulnerabilities, such as injection attacks like SQL injection or cross-site scripting (XSS). Authentication and authorization are integral components of software security. Authentication verifies the identity of users or components attempting to access the application, while authorization determines what actions or resources they are allowed to access. Implementing strong authentication and authorization mechanisms helps prevent unauthorized access and data breaches. Secure coding practices are fundamental to software security. Developers should follow industry-standard guidelines and best practices for writing secure code, including avoiding insecure functions, validating data, and using encryption where appropriate. Secure coding practices also involve addressing common vulnerabilities, such as buffer overflows and memory leaks, which can lead to security breaches. Secure software development lifecycle (SDLC) is a key concept in software security. It involves integrating security measures and assessments into every phase of the software development process, from design and coding to testing and deployment. By incorporating security from the outset, organizations can identify and address vulnerabilities early, reducing the cost and effort required to remediate issues later in the development cycle. Security testing and assessment play a crucial role in software security. These activities involve thoroughly evaluating an application's security posture through techniques such as penetration testing, code reviews, and static and dynamic analysis. Security testing helps uncover vulnerabilities and weaknesses that may not be apparent through regular code reviews or design inspections. Encryption is a fundamental tool for protecting sensitive data in software applications. It involves converting plaintext data into ciphertext using encryption algorithms and cryptographic keys. Encryption helps safeguard data both at rest and in transit, preventing unauthorized access and data breaches. Monitoring and logging are essential for detecting and responding to security incidents. Software applications should generate logs that capture relevant security-related events and activities. Monitoring and analyzing these logs enable organizations to identify anomalies, detect security incidents, and respond promptly to security breaches. Incident response planning is a critical component of software security fundamentals. Organizations should develop and maintain an incident response plan that outlines the steps to take when a security incident occurs. This plan should include procedures for containment, eradication, recovery, and communication. Software security is an ongoing process that requires continuous improvement and adaptation. As new threats and vulnerabilities emerge, organizations must update their security measures to address these challenges. Security patches and updates should be applied promptly to address known vulnerabilities and maintain the security of software systems. Security awareness and training are essential for all individuals involved in software development and maintenance. Developers, testers, and administrators should receive training on secure coding practices, threat mitigation techniques, and security best practices. By raising awareness and fostering a security-conscious culture, organizations can reduce the likelihood of security breaches caused by human error. In summary, software security fundamentals form the cornerstone of protecting software applications from threats and vulnerabilities. Understanding concepts such as threat modeling, least privilege, input validation, authentication, authorization, secure coding practices, secure SDLC, security testing, encryption, monitoring, incident response planning, and security awareness is essential for building robust and resilient software systems. By integrating these fundamentals into software development and maintenance processes, organizations can enhance the security and integrity of their software applications in an increasingly interconnected and digital world.

Proactive security measures are a critical aspect of cybersecurity that organizations should embrace to enhance their defense against evolving threats and vulnerabilities. Rather than reacting to security incidents after they occur, proactive security focuses on anticipating and preventing potential threats, making it an essential part of any robust cybersecurity strategy. One key proactive security measure is the implementation of a comprehensive security policy. A well-defined security policy outlines an organization's security objectives, expectations, and rules, serving as a foundation for all security efforts. This policy should address various aspects of security, such as data protection, access controls, incident response, and employee responsibilities. It sets the tone for the organization's commitment to security and serves as a reference for employees and stakeholders. Employee training and awareness programs are essential in proactive security. The human factor plays a significant role in cybersecurity, as employees are often the first line of defense against social engineering attacks and phishing attempts. Regular training programs educate employees about security best practices, common threats, and how to recognize and respond to suspicious activities. This proactive approach helps reduce the likelihood of security breaches caused by human error. Vulnerability assessments and penetration testing are proactive measures aimed at identifying and addressing security weaknesses. Vulnerability assessments involve systematically scanning systems and networks to uncover potential vulnerabilities. Penetration testing goes a step further by simulating real-world attacks to assess the organization's security posture. Both methods provide valuable insights into an organization's security gaps and areas that require improvement. Implementing proactive monitoring and threat detection systems is crucial for identifying and responding to security threats in real-time. These systems continuously monitor network traffic, system logs, and user activities to detect unusual or suspicious behavior. When anomalies are detected, security teams can take immediate action to investigate and mitigate potential threats before they escalate. Proactive security also involves the regular patching and updating of software and systems. Outdated software is a common target for attackers, as it may contain known vulnerabilities. By staying current with software patches and updates, organizations can close security gaps and reduce the risk of exploitation. Security incident response planning is a critical proactive measure. While organizations strive to prevent security incidents, they must also prepare for the possibility of a breach. An incident response plan outlines the steps to take when a security incident occurs, including containment, eradication, recovery, and communication. Proactive planning ensures that security teams can respond swiftly and effectively to minimize the impact of incidents. Security audits and assessments help organizations proactively evaluate their security posture. These assessments can be conducted internally or by third-party experts and involve reviewing security policies, practices, and controls. Audits identify areas of improvement and compliance with security standards and regulations. Encryption is a proactive measure for protecting sensitive data. Data encryption ensures that data remains confidential even if it falls into the wrong hands. Proactive encryption efforts encompass both data at rest (stored data) and data in transit (data being transmitted between systems). Establishing strong access controls is fundamental in proactive security. Access controls determine who can access specific resources and what actions they can perform. Implementing the principle of least privilege ensures that users and systems have the minimum level of access necessary to perform their tasks, reducing the attack surface. Regular security assessments and red teaming exercises are proactive approaches to test an organization's security defenses. Red teaming involves hiring external experts to simulate cyberattacks and identify vulnerabilities that may not be apparent through regular testing. These exercises provide a real-world assessment of an organization's security readiness. Proactive security measures should also include continuous monitoring and improvement. Threats and vulnerabilities evolve, so organizations must adapt their security measures accordingly. This involves staying informed about emerging threats, conducting regular security assessments, and revising security policies and practices as needed. Regularly reviewing and updating the incident response plan ensures that it remains effective in addressing new types of security incidents. In summary, proactive security measures are essential for organizations seeking to fortify their cybersecurity defenses. These measures encompass various aspects, including security policies, employee training, vulnerability assessments, monitoring and detection, patch management, incident response planning, audits and assessments, encryption, access controls, and continuous improvement. By embracing proactive security measures, organizations can better anticipate, prevent, and respond to security threats, reducing the risk of security breaches and protecting their valuable assets in an ever-evolving threat landscape.

Chapter 10: Becoming a Novice Vulnerability Analyst

Transitioning into vulnerability analysis can be an exciting and rewarding career move for those passionate about cybersecurity. Vulnerability analysts play a crucial role in identifying, assessing, and mitigating security vulnerabilities that could pose risks to organizations. As you embark on this journey, it's essential to understand the key aspects of vulnerability analysis and how to navigate this challenging but fulfilling field. First and foremost, vulnerability analysts need to build a strong foundation in information security. A solid understanding of cybersecurity principles, concepts, and best practices is vital. This knowledge will serve as the bedrock upon which you'll develop your expertise in vulnerability analysis. To start, consider pursuing relevant certifications such as Certified Information Systems Security Professional (CISSP) or Certified Ethical Hacker (CEH). These certifications provide a comprehensive overview of cybersecurity and will help you gain essential knowledge. Next, familiarize yourself with the tools and techniques commonly used in vulnerability analysis. There is a wide range of vulnerability scanning and assessment tools available, each with its strengths and weaknesses. Some popular tools include Nessus, OpenVAS, and Qualys for automated scanning, and Wireshark and Burp Suite for manual analysis. Learning how to use these tools effectively is a critical step in your journey. Moreover, understand the different types of vulnerabilities and how they can be exploited. Common vulnerability categories include software vulnerabilities, network vulnerabilities, and configuration vulnerabilities. Each type requires a unique approach to identification and mitigation. Software vulnerabilities, for example, often involve analyzing code for weaknesses, while network vulnerabilities may require extensive scanning and probing. Configuration vulnerabilities can result from improper system configurations, which need to be identified and remediated. Vulnerability analysts should also develop strong analytical and problem-solving skills. Analyzing complex systems, identifying vulnerabilities, and assessing their impact require a methodical and logical approach. You'll need to think critically and creatively to uncover vulnerabilities that malicious actors might exploit. Communication skills are equally important for a vulnerability analyst. You'll be responsible for communicating your findings and recommendations to various stakeholders, including IT teams, developers, and management. Being able to convey technical information in a clear and understandable manner is a valuable skill. In addition to technical skills, ethical considerations are paramount in vulnerability analysis. As a vulnerability analyst, you'll be entrusted with sensitive information about an organization's security posture. It's essential to adhere to ethical guidelines and maintain the highest level of integrity. Never engage in any malicious activities or unauthorized testing that could harm systems or networks. Instead, always follow ethical hacking practices and seek proper authorization when conducting assessments. Another critical aspect of vulnerability analysis is staying current with the ever-evolving threat landscape. Cyber threats are continually changing, and new vulnerabilities emerge regularly. Therefore, continuous learning and staying informed about the latest security developments are essential. Subscribe to security news sources, attend conferences, and participate in relevant online communities to keep your knowledge up to date. Networking within the cybersecurity community can be immensely beneficial. Building relationships with fellow professionals, sharing experiences, and seeking mentorship can accelerate your growth in vulnerability analysis. Mentors can provide valuable insights, guidance, and real-world perspectives that textbooks and courses may not cover. Hands-on experience is a vital component of becoming a skilled vulnerability analyst. Practice is key, and you can start by setting up a lab environment to experiment with various tools and techniques safely. Consider creating your own vulnerable applications or systems to practice identifying and exploiting vulnerabilities ethically. Engaging in capture the flag (CTF) competitions and challenges can also hone your skills. Furthermore, consider pursuing more advanced certifications specific to vulnerability analysis, such as the Certified Vulnerability Assessor (CVA) or Offensive Security Certified Professional (OSCP). These certifications delve deeper into the practical aspects of vulnerability analysis and ethical hacking. Once you've gained expertise and experience in vulnerability analysis, you can explore career opportunities in this field. Many organizations, including government agencies, financial institutions, and cybersecurity firms, hire vulnerability analysts to assess and improve their security posture. You may choose to work as an internal analyst within an organization's security team or as a consultant providing services to various clients. In either role, your skills will be in high demand as organizations seek to protect their digital assets from evolving threats. It's essential to continuously develop and refine your skills throughout your career. Consider specializing in specific areas of vulnerability analysis, such as web application security, network security, or cloud security. By becoming an expert in a particular domain, you can position yourself as a sought-after professional in the cybersecurity industry. In summary, transitioning into vulnerability analysis is an exciting and rewarding journey for those passionate about cybersecurity. Building a strong foundation in information security, mastering tools and techniques, developing analytical and communication skills, and adhering to ethical guidelines are essential steps in this process. Continuous learning, networking, hands-on experience, and advanced certifications will further your expertise. As a vulnerability analyst, you'll play a vital role in identifying and mitigating security vulnerabilities, helping organizations safeguard their digital assets in an ever-changing threat landscape.

Building skills for novice analysts is an essential step in preparing individuals for a career in cybersecurity.

Novice analysts, often at the beginning of their cybersecurity journey, need to acquire a strong foundation of knowledge and develop practical skills. This foundation will enable them to understand the intricacies of the field and contribute effectively to cybersecurity efforts. One of the first skills novice analysts should focus on is developing a comprehensive understanding of information security fundamentals. This includes learning about the core concepts, principles, and best practices that underpin the entire field of cybersecurity. Understanding topics such as threat modeling, risk assessment, access controls, and security policies is crucial for building a strong foundation. To acquire this knowledge, individuals can enroll in formal cybersecurity courses, read cybersecurity books and articles, or participate in online training programs. Practical experience is invaluable for novice analysts. Hands-on practice allows individuals to apply theoretical knowledge to real-world scenarios and develop critical thinking skills. Setting up a lab environment to experiment with various tools and techniques is an excellent way to gain practical experience. Creating vulnerable applications or systems for testing and experimentation can provide valuable insights into how vulnerabilities are exploited. Participating in capture the flag (CTF) competitions and cybersecurity challenges is another effective way to hone practical skills. Understanding network fundamentals is a critical skill for novice analysts. This includes grasping concepts like IP addressing, routing, subnetting, and network protocols. Network knowledge is essential for analyzing network traffic, identifying anomalies, and detecting potential security threats. To build these skills, individuals can study networking textbooks, take online networking courses, or pursue networking certifications like CompTIA Network+ or Cisco Certified Network Associate (CCNA). Another key area for novice analysts is learning about operating systems and their security. Different operating systems have various security features and vulnerabilities that analysts should be familiar with. Building a solid understanding of operating system fundamentals, including file systems, user management, and access controls, is essential. Additionally, novice analysts should explore common security mechanisms and configurations specific to different operating systems. Gaining proficiency in using security tools is essential for novice analysts. These tools help analysts assess and monitor security, identify vulnerabilities, and respond to security incidents. Some popular security tools include vulnerability scanners, intrusion detection systems, packet analyzers, and security information and event management (SIEM) solutions. Novice analysts should learn how to use these tools effectively through hands-on practice and training. Analytical skills are crucial for novice analysts, as they need to evaluate and interpret data to identify security threats and vulnerabilities. Developing the ability to think critically and analyze information from various sources is essential. This includes examining logs, network traffic, and system configurations to detect anomalies and potential security breaches. Communication skills are equally important for novice analysts. Being able to convey complex technical information in a clear and concise manner is essential when working with colleagues, superiors, and clients. Analysts often need to write reports, document findings, and communicate security incidents effectively. Practicing effective communication through written and verbal means is a valuable skill. Ethical considerations are fundamental for novice analysts. Maintaining ethical conduct and adhering to legal and professional standards is essential in the cybersecurity field. Novice analysts should be aware of the legal and ethical boundaries when conducting security assessments and handling sensitive information. Building a strong ethical foundation is crucial for a successful career in cybersecurity. Security awareness is an ongoing process for novice analysts. Cyber threats and attack techniques constantly evolve, so staying informed about the latest security developments is essential. Reading security news, blogs, and research papers can help analysts keep up to date with emerging threats. Participating in cybersecurity forums, attending conferences, and joining online communities are also effective ways to stay informed and connected with the cybersecurity community. Certifications can validate the skills and knowledge of novice analysts. There are several certifications in the cybersecurity field that can provide formal recognition of an individual's expertise. Certifications like CompTIA Security+, Certified Information Systems Security Professional (CISSP), and Certified Ethical Hacker (CEH) are well-respected in the industry and can boost a novice analyst's career prospects. Collaboration and teamwork are valuable skills for novice analysts. In many cybersecurity roles, analysts need to work closely with colleagues from various departments, including IT, legal, and compliance. Being able to collaborate effectively, share information, and contribute to a team's success is essential. In summary, building skills for novice analysts is a multifaceted journey that encompasses a wide range of knowledge and abilities. From information security fundamentals to practical experience, networking, operating systems, security tools, analytical and communication skills, ethical considerations, security awareness, certifications, and collaboration, novice analysts must develop a well-rounded skill set. This foundation prepares them to tackle the complex and ever-changing challenges of the cybersecurity field and contribute effectively to safeguarding digital assets and information in today's interconnected world.

BOOK 2
ZERO DAY EXPOSED
INTERMEDIATE TECHNIQUES FOR IDENTIFYING AND PATCHING SOFTWARE BUGS

ROB BOTWRIGHT

Chapter 1: Building on the Basics of Software Vulnerabilities

Recapping the fundamentals of software vulnerabilities is essential to lay a strong foundation for understanding the broader landscape of cybersecurity. Software vulnerabilities are weaknesses or flaws in software applications, operating systems, or hardware that can be exploited by attackers to compromise the security of a system. These vulnerabilities can manifest in various forms, from coding errors and design flaws to misconfigurations and human errors. Understanding the types of software vulnerabilities is crucial, as they come in many varieties. Common types include buffer overflows, SQL injection, cross-site scripting (XSS), and authentication bypass, among others. Each type of vulnerability poses unique risks and requires specific mitigation strategies. The impact of a software vulnerability can range from minor inconveniences to severe security breaches, depending on factors such as the nature of the vulnerability and the attacker's intent. In some cases, vulnerabilities can lead to unauthorized access, data theft, or even complete system compromise. Software vendors play a significant role in addressing vulnerabilities through the release of patches and updates. When vulnerabilities are discovered, vendors work to develop and release fixes to eliminate the weaknesses and protect users. However, it's crucial for organizations and individuals to apply these patches promptly to mitigate the risk of exploitation. A critical aspect of software vulnerabilities is responsible disclosure. When security researchers or ethical hackers discover vulnerabilities, they have an ethical obligation to report them to the affected vendors and give them a reasonable amount of time to develop fixes. This responsible approach helps protect users and allows vendors to address issues before they can be exploited maliciously. Vulnerability databases and repositories, such as the Common Vulnerabilities and Exposures (CVE) database, provide standardized and accessible information about known vulnerabilities. These databases enable organizations to track and manage vulnerabilities in their software and systems effectively. Another vital concept in software vulnerability management is the Common Vulnerability Scoring System (CVSS), which provides a standardized method for assessing the severity of vulnerabilities based on various factors. By assigning a CVSS score to vulnerabilities, organizations can prioritize which vulnerabilities to address first. The process of identifying vulnerabilities often involves both automated and manual methods. Vulnerability scanning tools, like Nessus or OpenVAS, automate the process by scanning systems and applications for known vulnerabilities. Manual code review and analysis, performed by security experts, delve into the source code to uncover vulnerabilities that automated tools might miss. Vulnerability management is an ongoing process that includes the identification, assessment, prioritization, and remediation of vulnerabilities. This process helps organizations systematically reduce their exposure to potential security risks. An essential aspect of vulnerability management is the development of effective remediation strategies. Once vulnerabilities are identified and prioritized, organizations need to determine the best course of action to mitigate the risks. Remediation can take various forms, from applying software patches and updates to reconfiguring systems and implementing security controls. Additionally, organizations should establish incident response plans to address vulnerabilities when they are actively exploited or when a security incident occurs. A crucial component of vulnerability management is the concept of a zero-day vulnerability. A zero-day vulnerability is a security flaw in software that is not yet known to the vendor or the public. This type of vulnerability can be particularly dangerous, as there are no patches or fixes available to protect against it. To address zero-day vulnerabilities, organizations need to implement proactive security measures, such as intrusion detection systems and network segmentation, to minimize the potential impact. Vulnerability analysis plays a central role in the identification and assessment of vulnerabilities. Security professionals and ethical hackers often conduct vulnerability assessments to evaluate the security posture of systems and applications. This process involves scanning, testing, and analyzing systems for vulnerabilities and weaknesses. The results of vulnerability assessments help organizations prioritize and remediate security issues. Ethical hacking, or penetration testing, is a practice where skilled professionals attempt to exploit vulnerabilities in a controlled and ethical manner to identify weaknesses that could be exploited maliciously. This approach helps organizations proactively uncover vulnerabilities before attackers can do so. In summary, understanding software vulnerability fundamentals is vital for anyone involved in cybersecurity. From the types of vulnerabilities and their impact to responsible disclosure, vulnerability databases, CVSS scoring, vulnerability management, remediation strategies, zero-day vulnerabilities, and vulnerability analysis, these fundamentals provide a comprehensive view of the cybersecurity landscape. By mastering these concepts, individuals and organizations can better protect their systems and data from the ever-present threat of software vulnerabilities and security breaches.

Advancing your understanding of vulnerabilities is a natural progression in your journey to becoming a seasoned cybersecurity professional. As you delve deeper into the world of vulnerabilities, you'll encounter more complex concepts and scenarios that demand a higher level of expertise. One of the first steps in advancing your understanding is gaining a comprehensive grasp of the different categories and classifications of vulnerabilities. While you may be familiar with common types like buffer overflows, SQL injection, and cross-site scripting (XSS), there are many more to explore. Vulnerabilities can be categorized based on their impact, exploitability, and the systems or applications they affect. Understanding these categories will help you assess and prioritize vulnerabilities effectively. Moreover, advanced vulnerability analysis involves a deeper exploration of exploit techniques. You'll learn how attackers manipulate vulnerabilities to gain unauthorized access, compromise systems, and achieve their objectives. This knowledge is essential for not only identifying vulnerabilities but also understanding the potential consequences of exploitation. Beyond the basics, you'll encounter advanced exploitation techniques that require a higher level of skill and expertise. These techniques often involve complex manipulation of memory, data structures, or system behaviors. By studying these advanced methods, you can gain insights into the intricacies of vulnerability exploitation. An essential aspect of advancing your understanding of vulnerabilities is delving into reverse engineering and binary analysis. Reverse engineering involves dissecting software binaries to understand their inner workings. This skill is invaluable for vulnerability analysts, as it enables them to analyze proprietary software and discover vulnerabilities that may not be apparent through source code analysis alone. Binary analysis also involves studying malware, a field that is becoming increasingly important in the ever-evolving threat landscape. Understanding malware behavior and analyzing its code is crucial for identifying vulnerabilities that may be exploited by malicious software. Vulnerability researchers often specialize in specific domains or technologies. For example, you may choose to focus on web application security, network security, IoT (Internet of Things) vulnerabilities, or cloud security. Specialization allows you to become an expert in a particular area and contribute more effectively to vulnerability analysis efforts. To advance your understanding in your chosen domain, you'll need to keep up with the latest developments and emerging threats specific to that area. Attending specialized conferences, reading research papers, and participating in relevant communities can help you stay at the forefront of your chosen field. Collaboration and sharing knowledge with your peers play a significant role in advancing your understanding of vulnerabilities. Engaging in discussions, exchanging insights, and participating in vulnerability research communities can expand your knowledge base and expose you to new ideas and approaches. Furthermore, consider pursuing advanced certifications and training programs that are specific to vulnerability analysis and exploitation. Certifications like Offensive Security Certified Expert (OSCE) and Certified Exploit Developer (CED) are designed to validate your expertise in these areas. As you advance, you'll encounter more sophisticated tools and frameworks that aid in vulnerability analysis and exploitation. Tools like Metasploit, IDA Pro, and Ghidra provide advanced capabilities for vulnerability researchers and ethical hackers. Learning how to use these tools effectively will enhance your capabilities and efficiency in identifying and exploiting vulnerabilities. Ethical hacking, often referred to as penetration testing, is a critical skill for advanced vulnerability analysts. Ethical hackers simulate real-world attacks to identify vulnerabilities and weaknesses in systems, networks, and applications. This practice requires a deep understanding of both offensive and defensive cybersecurity strategies. To become proficient in ethical hacking, consider pursuing certifications like Certified Ethical Hacker (CEH) and Offensive Security Certified Professional (OSCP). Ethical hackers often work in red teaming engagements, where they act as adversaries to assess an organization's security defenses. This advanced level of testing helps organizations identify and remediate vulnerabilities in a realistic and challenging environment. As you advance in your understanding of vulnerabilities, you'll become more adept at discovering zero-day vulnerabilities. Zero-day vulnerabilities are flaws in software or hardware that are unknown to the vendor or the public. These vulnerabilities can be particularly valuable to attackers, as there are no patches or fixes available to protect against them. Vulnerability researchers who discover and responsibly disclose zero-day vulnerabilities play a crucial role in enhancing cybersecurity. The process of responsible disclosure involves notifying the affected vendor and giving them time to develop and release a patch before the vulnerability is made public. This practice helps protect users and ensures that vulnerabilities are addressed without exposing systems to unnecessary risks. In summary, advancing your understanding of vulnerabilities is a journey that requires continuous learning, specialization, and the development of advanced skills. By exploring different vulnerability categories, mastering advanced exploitation techniques, delving into reverse engineering and binary analysis, specializing in specific domains, collaborating with peers, pursuing advanced certifications, mastering sophisticated tools, and becoming proficient in ethical hacking and zero-day vulnerability discovery, you can reach a high level of expertise in vulnerability analysis. This expertise is invaluable in the ever-evolving landscape of cybersecurity, where identifying and mitigating vulnerabilities is crucial to safeguarding digital assets and information.

Chapter 2: Diving Deeper into Vulnerability Analysis

Advanced techniques in vulnerability analysis represent the pinnacle of expertise in the field of cybersecurity. As you progress in your career and become a seasoned professional, you'll find that the ability to uncover and mitigate complex vulnerabilities becomes increasingly valuable. In this chapter, we'll explore some of the most advanced techniques employed by expert vulnerability analysts. One of the first advanced techniques to consider is fuzz testing, also known as fuzzing. Fuzzing involves systematically injecting malformed or unexpected data into software applications to discover vulnerabilities. This method can uncover obscure vulnerabilities that might not be apparent through conventional testing. Fuzzing tools and frameworks like American Fuzzy Lop (AFL) and libFuzzer have gained popularity for their effectiveness in identifying software flaws. Beyond traditional fuzzing, you can delve into protocol-level fuzzing, where you analyze the behavior of network protocols. Protocol-level fuzzing can reveal vulnerabilities in network services, leading to more secure networked applications. Advanced vulnerability analysts often specialize in web application security. To excel in this domain, it's essential to master techniques like manual code review and dynamic analysis. Manual code review involves a thorough examination of an application's source code to identify vulnerabilities that automated tools may miss. Dynamic analysis, on the other hand, focuses on the runtime behavior of web applications. Tools like Burp Suite and OWASP ZAP assist analysts in intercepting and manipulating web traffic, allowing them to identify security issues in real-time. An important aspect of web application security is understanding and exploiting authentication and authorization vulnerabilities. This includes techniques such as session fixation, privilege escalation, and bypassing access controls. These advanced techniques require a deep understanding of web application architecture and the ability to identify and exploit vulnerabilities effectively. As you advance in vulnerability analysis, you'll encounter complex authentication mechanisms like multi-factor authentication (MFA) and single sign-on (SSO). Understanding these systems and their potential weaknesses is crucial for assessing the security of modern web applications. You may also delve into the realm of identity and access management (IAM), where you analyze how organizations manage user identities and permissions. Advanced IAM attacks may involve identity spoofing, token manipulation, and the abuse of federation and trust relationships. Mastering these techniques requires a deep understanding of IAM protocols and architectures. Network security remains a critical focus for advanced vulnerability analysts. Intricate techniques such as network traffic analysis and protocol exploitation become essential skills in this domain. Network traffic analysis involves dissecting network packets to identify anomalies and potential vulnerabilities. Tools like Wireshark and tcpdump are invaluable for inspecting network traffic and understanding communication patterns. Additionally, protocol exploitation involves identifying weaknesses in network protocols and exploiting them to compromise systems or intercept sensitive data. Advanced analysts may even engage in protocol-level attacks like DNS poisoning or BGP hijacking. For those who specialize in IoT security, advanced techniques are necessary to assess the security of connected devices. IoT devices often lack standard security measures, making them attractive targets for attackers. Reverse engineering firmware, analyzing device communication protocols, and conducting hardware assessments are advanced skills in IoT security. Reverse engineering firmware allows analysts to understand the inner workings of IoT devices and uncover vulnerabilities. Analyzing device communication protocols involves intercepting and decoding the data exchanged between IoT devices and backend servers. Hardware assessments, on the other hand, may require specialized equipment to examine the physical components of IoT devices for vulnerabilities. Cloud security is another domain where advanced vulnerability analysts can make a significant impact. As organizations increasingly migrate to cloud environments, understanding the security challenges unique to cloud computing becomes crucial. Advanced techniques in cloud security include analyzing cloud configurations, identifying misconfigurations, and assessing the security of cloud APIs. Cloud configuration analysis involves evaluating an organization's cloud settings to ensure they align with best practices. Misconfigurations can expose sensitive data or provide attackers with unauthorized access. Assessing cloud APIs is essential for identifying potential vulnerabilities that could be exploited to compromise cloud services. Advanced vulnerability analysts also need to stay current with emerging cloud security threats and trends.

Containerization and container security have gained prominence in recent years, with technologies like Docker and Kubernetes becoming ubiquitous. Advanced analysts may specialize in container security, which involves assessing the security of containerized applications and orchestrating platforms. Techniques such as container image analysis, runtime security, and Kubernetes exploitation are essential for evaluating containerized environments. Container image analysis includes scanning container images for known vulnerabilities and ensuring that they adhere to security best practices. Runtime security focuses on monitoring container behavior and detecting anomalous activities. Kubernetes exploitation requires an understanding of Kubernetes architecture and the ability to identify and exploit misconfigurations or vulnerabilities within Kubernetes clusters. Another advanced area of vulnerability analysis is the study of advanced persistent threats (APTs). APTs are sophisticated, long-term cyberattacks orchestrated by well-funded and determined adversaries. Analyzing APTs requires an in-depth understanding of malware, advanced attack techniques, and threat actor behavior. Advanced vulnerability analysts often engage in threat intelligence activities to monitor and analyze APT campaigns, identify indicators of compromise (IoCs), and assess the tactics, techniques, and procedures (TTPs) employed by threat actors. This information helps organizations better defend against APTs and enhance their cybersecurity posture. In summary, advancing your understanding of vulnerabilities to an expert level involves mastering a wide range of advanced techniques and specializing in specific domains of cybersecurity. Fuzz testing, web application security, authentication and authorization vulnerabilities, identity and access management, network security, IoT security, cloud security, container security, and APT analysis are all areas where advanced vulnerability analysts excel. Continuously expanding your knowledge, staying up to date with emerging threats, and honing your skills are essential to becoming a trusted expert in vulnerability analysis, capable of protecting organizations from evolving cyber threats.

Analyzing vulnerabilities with precision is a hallmark of expertise in the field of cybersecurity. As a seasoned vulnerability analyst, your ability to delve deeply into the intricacies of vulnerabilities sets you apart. Precision in vulnerability analysis involves a systematic and meticulous approach to identifying, understanding, and mitigating security weaknesses. One of the key aspects of precise vulnerability analysis is comprehensive knowledge of various operating systems. You must be well-versed in the inner workings of Windows, Linux, macOS, and other operating systems commonly used in enterprise environments. This knowledge allows you to assess vulnerabilities specific to each operating system and understand their potential impact. Moreover, precise vulnerability analysis requires a deep understanding of system internals. You must be capable of analyzing system memory, file structures, and system calls to identify vulnerabilities hidden within the operating system. This level of expertise enables you to uncover subtle flaws that might elude less-experienced analysts. Beyond operating systems, you must also possess a thorough understanding of application-level vulnerabilities. Web applications, in particular, are a common target for attackers, making web application security a critical domain for precise analysis. To analyze web applications with precision, you need to be proficient in various programming languages, including HTML, JavaScript, PHP, and Python. You should also understand how web frameworks operate and be able to scrutinize source code for vulnerabilities like SQL injection, XSS, CSRF, and insecure authentication mechanisms. Precision in vulnerability analysis goes hand in hand with reverse engineering skills. Reverse engineering allows you to dissect binaries, examine compiled code, and understand how software functions at the lowest level. You might reverse engineer malware to understand its behavior or analyze proprietary software to identify vulnerabilities. To excel in reverse engineering, you must be proficient in tools like IDA Pro and Ghidra, which assist in disassembling and decompiling code. Network protocols and packet analysis are another area where precision is crucial. You need to be adept at using tools like Wireshark to capture and dissect network traffic. Analyzing packet captures with precision enables you to identify suspicious or malicious activity and pinpoint potential vulnerabilities in networked systems. Furthermore, understanding cryptographic principles and cryptographic vulnerabilities is essential. Cryptography plays a pivotal role in securing systems and data, but vulnerabilities in cryptographic implementations can be subtle and challenging to detect. Precise analysis involves scrutinizing cryptographic algorithms, key management, and encryption protocols to identify weaknesses that could lead to security breaches. Throughout the vulnerability analysis process, you must maintain meticulous records. Detailed documentation is not only important for your own reference but also for communication with colleagues, superiors, and clients. Precise documentation ensures that your findings are clear, reproducible, and actionable. It includes detailed notes on the vulnerability's characteristics, how it was identified, potential exploits, and recommended remediation steps. Vulnerability databases, such as the Common Vulnerabilities and Exposures (CVE) database, are valuable resources for precise analysis. These databases provide standardized information about known vulnerabilities, including their severity and impact. Using CVE identifiers in your documentation helps establish a common language for discussing vulnerabilities within the cybersecurity community. Moreover, precise vulnerability analysis involves continuous learning and staying up to date with emerging threats. The cybersecurity landscape is constantly evolving, with new vulnerabilities and attack techniques emerging regularly. To maintain precision in your analysis, you must keep abreast of the latest developments, security patches, and threat intelligence. Participating in cybersecurity forums, attending conferences, and engaging with the security community are effective ways to stay informed and exchange knowledge with peers. Ethical considerations are paramount in vulnerability analysis. Maintaining ethical conduct and adhering to legal and professional standards is non-negotiable. Precise vulnerability analysts prioritize responsible disclosure, ensuring that vulnerabilities are reported to vendors and the appropriate authorities in a timely and ethical manner. This practice protects users and allows vendors to develop patches before malicious actors can exploit the vulnerabilities. A critical aspect of precise vulnerability analysis is the ability to assess the business impact of vulnerabilities. You should be able to evaluate not only the technical aspects of a vulnerability but also its potential consequences on an organization's operations, data, and reputation. Understanding the context in which a vulnerability exists helps organizations prioritize remediation efforts effectively. Effective communication is vital for precise vulnerability analysis. You must convey your findings and recommendations clearly and concisely to both technical and non-technical stakeholders. This includes writing comprehensive reports and providing briefings that enable decision-makers to understand the risks and take appropriate actions. Additionally, you may need to educate and train others in your organization on best practices for vulnerability management. In summary, analyzing vulnerabilities with precision is the hallmark of an expert vulnerability analyst. It involves in-depth knowledge of operating systems, system internals, web application security, reverse engineering, network protocols, cryptography, meticulous documentation, reliance on vulnerability databases, continuous learning, ethical considerations, assessing business impact, effective communication, and educating others. Precision in vulnerability analysis ensures that security weaknesses are identified accurately and mitigated effectively, ultimately contributing to the protection of digital assets and information in an ever-evolving and interconnected world.

Chapter 3: Intermediate Exploitation Techniques

Advancing your exploitation skills is a crucial aspect of becoming a proficient cybersecurity professional. Exploitation, in the context of cybersecurity, refers to the process of leveraging vulnerabilities to compromise systems, gain unauthorized access, or achieve specific objectives. As you progress in your career, you'll find that having advanced exploitation skills is essential for both offensive and defensive cybersecurity roles. One of the fundamental skills in exploitation is understanding the techniques used to compromise vulnerable systems. This includes methods like buffer overflows, SQL injection, and privilege escalation. Buffer overflows, for example, involve overwriting memory areas to execute arbitrary code, a technique often used to take control of a system. Advanced exploitation skills require a deep understanding of how these techniques work at the low-level, including the manipulation of memory addresses and registers. In addition to the basics, advanced exploitation often involves studying and exploiting zero-day vulnerabilities. Zero-day vulnerabilities are security flaws that are unknown to the software vendor and the public. Because there are no patches or fixes available, they are highly sought after by attackers. Advanced exploit developers and vulnerability analysts specialize in discovering and exploiting zero-day vulnerabilities. This process involves extensive research, reverse engineering, and creative thinking to develop reliable exploits. To advance your exploitation skills, you'll need to become proficient in reverse engineering. Reverse engineering is the process of analyzing software binaries or hardware components to understand how they work. For software exploitation, this skill is invaluable as it allows you to dissect proprietary applications or malware to discover vulnerabilities and develop exploits. Reverse engineering tools like IDA Pro, Ghidra, and Radare2 are commonly used in this process. Another area of focus for advanced exploitation is web application security. Web applications are a prime target for attackers, and understanding how to exploit vulnerabilities like SQL injection, cross-site scripting (XSS), and remote code execution is crucial. Advanced web application exploitation involves bypassing security mechanisms, chaining multiple vulnerabilities together, and manipulating input data creatively to achieve desired outcomes. In addition to web application exploitation, advanced analysts may specialize in network exploitation. Network exploitation involves compromising networked systems or services to gain access or control. This can include exploiting vulnerabilities in network protocols, routers, or services running on servers. Sophisticated attackers may engage in protocol-level attacks like DNS poisoning or man-in-the-middle (MitM) attacks. Advanced network exploitation skills also encompass post-exploitation activities, such as lateral movement within a network and privilege escalation on compromised systems. A key aspect of advancing your exploitation skills is keeping up with the latest attack techniques and evasion tactics. The cybersecurity landscape is dynamic, and new exploitation methods emerge regularly. To stay current, you should engage with the cybersecurity community, read research papers, attend conferences, and participate in capture the flag (CTF) competitions or bug bounty programs. These activities provide practical experience and exposure to real-world attack scenarios. Ethical hacking or penetration testing is a valuable way to refine your exploitation skills in a controlled environment. Engaging in authorized and legal hacking activities allows you to practice exploitation techniques on target systems to identify vulnerabilities. Certifications like the Offensive Security Certified Professional (OSCP) and Certified Ethical Hacker (CEH) are well-regarded in the industry and require hands-on experience with exploitation. Advanced exploitation also involves developing custom payloads and shellcode. Payloads are pieces of code that are injected into a vulnerable system to carry out malicious actions, such as establishing a reverse shell for remote access. Creating custom payloads tailored to specific vulnerabilities and environments requires advanced coding skills and an understanding of exploit development. For example, developing shellcode for different operating systems or processor architectures demands expertise in assembly language programming. An important ethical consideration in advanced exploitation is responsible disclosure. When you discover vulnerabilities, it's essential to follow ethical guidelines and report them to the affected parties in a responsible and coordinated manner. Responsible disclosure gives vendors the opportunity to develop patches and protect their users before attackers can exploit the vulnerabilities. In advanced exploitation, you may also encounter ethical dilemmas related to offensive cybersecurity roles. These roles involve simulating real-world attacks, and ethical hackers must carefully consider the potential consequences of their actions. Clear rules of engagement, strong ethical guidelines, and strict adherence to legal and ethical standards are crucial in such roles. In summary, advancing your exploitation skills is a vital part of excelling in the cybersecurity field. Whether you're an offensive security professional, vulnerability analyst, or defensive security expert, understanding and mastering advanced exploitation techniques is essential. It requires in-depth knowledge of vulnerability exploitation, reverse engineering, zero-day research, web application and network exploitation, post-exploitation activities, staying current with evolving threats, engaging in ethical hacking, developing custom payloads and shellcode, and adhering to responsible disclosure practices. With these advanced skills, you can contribute effectively to securing digital assets and defending against evolving cyber threats in an ever-changing digital landscape.

Exploring intermediate-level exploitation scenarios is an exciting and essential part of your journey to becoming a proficient cybersecurity professional. Intermediate-level exploitation involves more complex and advanced techniques than basic exploitation but is not as specialized as advanced exploitation. By delving into these scenarios, you'll develop a deeper understanding of how attackers can compromise systems and, in turn, enhance your defensive capabilities. One of the key areas of intermediate-level exploitation is privilege escalation. Privilege escalation refers to the process of gaining higher-level access or permissions on a system or network than initially granted. Attackers often seek to escalate their privileges to perform actions that would otherwise be restricted. Understanding privilege escalation techniques is crucial for both offensive and defensive roles. Intermediate-level privilege escalation scenarios may involve exploiting misconfigured system services, weak access controls, or vulnerabilities in software. You'll learn to identify and exploit these weaknesses to elevate your privileges on a target system. Post-exploitation activities are another significant aspect of intermediate-level exploitation. Once an attacker gains initial access to a system, they typically aim to establish persistence, move laterally within the network, and maintain control over compromised systems. You'll explore techniques such as creating backdoors, disguising malicious activities, and evading detection mechanisms. These skills are essential for understanding the full scope of a cyberattack and defending against it effectively. Advanced exploitation of web applications is another exciting intermediate-level scenario. You'll delve into techniques like advanced SQL injection, blind SQL injection, and XML external entity (XXE) attacks. Advanced SQL injection involves exploiting SQL vulnerabilities to extract, modify, or delete sensitive data from a web application's database. Blind SQL injection is a more challenging variant where attackers infer the results of their injections indirectly. XXE attacks target XML parsers, allowing attackers to read sensitive files and execute arbitrary code. Understanding and defending against these advanced web application exploits is essential for securing online services. Intermediate-level exploitation scenarios often require a solid understanding of network protocols and communication. You'll learn to manipulate network traffic and exploit weaknesses in protocols. This includes techniques like ARP spoofing, DNS spoofing, and session hijacking. ARP spoofing involves redirecting network traffic to an attacker-controlled system, allowing for eavesdropping or man-in-the-middle attacks. DNS spoofing manipulates DNS responses to redirect users to malicious websites. Session hijacking can compromise user sessions and allow attackers to impersonate legitimate users. These network exploitation skills provide valuable insights into potential vulnerabilities and attack vectors. Advanced social engineering and phishing are also part of intermediate-level exploitation. You'll explore techniques to craft convincing phishing emails, conduct pretexting, and manipulate human behavior to gather information or gain access to systems. Social engineering attacks often exploit the weakest link in the cybersecurity chain—humans. Understanding these techniques is essential for both red teaming (offensive) and user awareness training (defensive) purposes.

Another intermediate-level scenario involves bypassing security mechanisms. This includes evading antivirus software, intrusion detection systems (IDS), and security policies. You'll explore methods to obfuscate malicious code, create custom payloads, and employ encryption to bypass security measures. Bypassing security mechanisms is essential for offensive security professionals seeking to avoid detection. As you explore intermediate-level exploitation scenarios, you'll encounter various tools and frameworks commonly used in offensive cybersecurity. Tools like Metasploit, Cobalt Strike, and Burp Suite are invaluable for penetration testing and exploitation. Metasploit, for instance, provides a range of exploits, payloads, and post-exploitation modules. Cobalt Strike offers advanced post-exploitation capabilities and collaborative features. Burp Suite assists in web application security testing and exploitation. These tools empower you to practice and refine your exploitation skills in controlled environments. Ethical considerations are paramount in intermediate-level exploitation scenarios. Responsible disclosure of vulnerabilities, adherence to legal and ethical guidelines, and maintaining a code of ethics are essential. Ethical hackers must ensure that their activities align with the law and ethical standards, even when conducting penetration tests or red teaming exercises. Developing a strong ethical foundation is essential for building a trustworthy career in cybersecurity. In summary, exploring intermediate-level exploitation scenarios is a critical step in your cybersecurity journey. These scenarios encompass privilege escalation, post-exploitation activities, advanced web application exploitation, network exploitation, social engineering, security mechanism bypass, and the use of specialized tools and frameworks. Ethical considerations, responsible disclosure, and a commitment to ethical conduct are integral to your growth as a cybersecurity professional. By mastering intermediate-level exploitation, you'll gain the knowledge and skills needed to protect systems and networks effectively while understanding the techniques employed by malicious actors.

Chapter 4: Zero Day Research and Discovery

The art of zero day discovery is a complex and highly specialized field within the realm of cybersecurity. Zero day vulnerabilities are software flaws that are unknown to the vendor and have no available patches. Discovering these vulnerabilities is a challenging endeavor that requires a unique skill set and a deep understanding of software and system internals. Zero day vulnerabilities pose significant risks to organizations and individuals as they can be exploited by malicious actors to compromise systems and data. The process of zero day discovery typically begins with extensive research and reconnaissance. Cybersecurity researchers and vulnerability analysts actively seek out potential targets for vulnerability analysis. This may involve identifying popular software applications, operating systems, or networked services that are likely to have undiscovered vulnerabilities. Once potential targets are identified, researchers delve into the software's code and architecture. This phase of discovery requires a keen eye for detail, as vulnerabilities often hide in the intricate codebase of complex software. Researchers may use static code analysis tools, dynamic analysis techniques, and even manual code review to identify suspicious patterns or code constructs that could lead to vulnerabilities. Understanding software architecture is essential in the zero day discovery process. Researchers must comprehend how different components of a software application interact and communicate with each other.

This knowledge helps in identifying potential weak points where vulnerabilities might be lurking. During the discovery process, researchers also examine the software's attack surface. This refers to the various entry points or interfaces through which an attacker might exploit a vulnerability. Common attack surfaces include network interfaces, input validation mechanisms, and APIs (Application Programming Interfaces). By thoroughly examining the attack surface, researchers can focus their efforts on areas most likely to contain vulnerabilities. Another critical aspect of zero day discovery is fuzz testing or fuzzing. Fuzzing involves sending malformed or unexpected data inputs to a software application to trigger potential vulnerabilities. This technique can uncover memory corruption issues, input validation flaws, and other types of software vulnerabilities. Fuzz testing can be automated, allowing researchers to systematically test different aspects of the software. In the quest for zero day vulnerabilities, researchers often resort to reverse engineering. Reverse engineering involves dissecting binary executables or firmware to understand how software functions at the lowest level. This skill is crucial for identifying vulnerabilities in closed-source or proprietary software. Reverse engineering tools like IDA Pro and Ghidra help researchers analyze binaries and uncover vulnerabilities. Additionally, zero day discovery often involves network traffic analysis. By examining network packets and communication patterns between software components, researchers can identify potential vulnerabilities related to data transmission and handling. In some cases, zero day vulnerabilities may be discovered through a combination of techniques, such as analyzing crash reports, monitoring system logs, and examining memory dumps. Zero day vulnerabilities come in various forms, including buffer overflows, privilege escalation flaws, race conditions, and logic errors. Researchers must be versatile in their approach to identifying these vulnerabilities. Once a potential zero day vulnerability is identified, researchers must validate its existence and impact. This involves creating proof-of-concept exploits to demonstrate how an attacker could leverage the vulnerability to compromise a system or gain unauthorized access. Validating the impact of a vulnerability is crucial for accurately assessing its severity and the level of risk it poses. Once a zero day vulnerability is confirmed and its impact assessed, responsible disclosure becomes a critical consideration. Researchers must decide how to report the vulnerability to the affected software vendor while minimizing the risk of exploitation by malicious actors. Ethical considerations are paramount in this process, as disclosing a zero day vulnerability responsibly ensures that users are protected. Some researchers choose to follow a responsible disclosure process, which involves notifying the vendor and providing them with sufficient time to develop and release a patch before making the vulnerability public. Others may work with third-party organizations or government agencies to facilitate the disclosure process. In rare cases, vulnerabilities may be sold to vendors, security companies, or government agencies through bug bounty programs or private sales. The art of zero day discovery requires continuous learning and adaptability. As software evolves and new technologies emerge, the techniques and tools used in vulnerability discovery must also evolve. Researchers must stay current with the latest developments in software and cybersecurity to remain effective in their pursuit of zero day vulnerabilities. Moreover, building a strong ethical foundation is essential, as the responsible disclosure of vulnerabilities is a fundamental ethical obligation in this field. In summary, the art of zero day discovery is a complex and dynamic field that plays a crucial role in enhancing cybersecurity. It involves extensive research, code analysis, system understanding, fuzz testing, reverse engineering, network traffic analysis, and responsible disclosure. Zero day vulnerabilities can have significant consequences, making the work of researchers and analysts in this area invaluable for protecting systems and data from potential threats.

Strategies for effective zero day research are fundamental to discovering and addressing vulnerabilities in software. Zero day vulnerabilities are a significant threat as they can be exploited by malicious actors before the software vendor releases a patch. To combat this threat, researchers and cybersecurity professionals employ various strategies and approaches to proactively identify and mitigate these vulnerabilities. One of the key strategies in effective zero day research is keeping a keen eye on software and system updates. Software vendors regularly release patches and updates to fix known vulnerabilities. By monitoring these updates, researchers can analyze the changes made to the software and identify potential vulnerabilities that were patched. This "patch diffing" technique is a valuable way to discover previously unknown vulnerabilities. Zero day research also involves analyzing historical data and trends. Researchers often study past zero day vulnerabilities to identify patterns, common attack vectors, and the types of software that are frequently targeted. This historical analysis can help researchers anticipate where future vulnerabilities may arise. Open-source intelligence (OSINT) is another critical component of effective zero day research. Researchers gather information from public sources such as forums, mailing lists, and social media to identify discussions or indicators related to potential zero day vulnerabilities. This proactive approach can lead to the early discovery of vulnerabilities before they are actively exploited. Furthermore, researchers frequently engage in vulnerability scanning and analysis. Automated tools and scanners are used to assess the security of software and systems for known vulnerabilities. By regularly scanning systems and applications, researchers can identify weaknesses that may be leveraged by attackers. Reverse engineering is a crucial skill in zero day research. Researchers often analyze the binary code of software applications to uncover vulnerabilities that are not apparent in the source code. Reverse engineering tools like IDA Pro, Ghidra, and Radare2 aid in dissecting software binaries. In-depth code analysis reveals potential weaknesses and vulnerabilities that may be exploited. Researchers also actively participate in capture the flag (CTF) competitions and bug bounty programs. These activities provide practical experience in vulnerability discovery and exploitation. CTF challenges simulate real-world scenarios, while bug bounty programs offer financial incentives for finding and responsibly disclosing vulnerabilities. Both avenues enhance researchers' skills and expertise. Effective zero day research requires a collaborative approach. Researchers often work with peers and share information within the cybersecurity community. Collaboration facilitates knowledge sharing, increases the speed of vulnerability discovery, and enhances the overall security posture of the community. Moreover, collaboration with vendors is crucial in responsible vulnerability disclosure. Researchers must establish communication channels with software vendors to report vulnerabilities and work together to develop patches. This cooperation ensures that vulnerabilities are addressed promptly to protect users. Automation is an increasingly important strategy in zero day research. Researchers use scripts and tools to automate various aspects of vulnerability discovery, such as data collection, analysis, and validation. Automation accelerates the research process and enables researchers to focus on more complex tasks. Machine learning and artificial intelligence are also emerging in zero day research. These technologies can analyze vast amounts of data to detect unusual patterns or behavior that may indicate a zero day vulnerability. Machine learning algorithms can help researchers identify anomalies in software behavior and reduce false positives. Effective zero day research requires a commitment to responsible disclosure. Researchers must follow ethical guidelines and legal standards when disclosing vulnerabilities to software vendors. Responsible disclosure ensures that vendors have the opportunity to develop and release patches before the vulnerability becomes public knowledge. Ethical considerations are paramount, as researchers have a duty to protect users and systems. Furthermore, it is essential to prioritize the severity of vulnerabilities. Not all vulnerabilities are created equal, and researchers must assess the potential impact of a zero day vulnerability. By focusing on the most critical vulnerabilities, researchers can ensure that their efforts are directed where they will have the most significant impact. Zero day research is an ongoing process. Researchers must continuously monitor the evolving threat landscape, adapt their strategies, and stay up-to-date with emerging technologies and attack vectors. By remaining vigilant and proactive, researchers play a vital role in enhancing cybersecurity and protecting systems from potential threats. In summary, effective zero day research is a multifaceted endeavor that combines monitoring software updates, historical analysis, open-source intelligence, vulnerability scanning, reverse engineering, participation in CTF competitions and bug bounty programs, collaboration, automation, responsible disclosure, ethical considerations, severity assessment, and ongoing vigilance. These strategies collectively empower researchers to discover and address zero day vulnerabilities, ultimately strengthening the security of software and systems.

Chapter 5: Vulnerability Assessment Tools for Intermediate Users

Leveraging intermediate-level assessment tools is a critical aspect of vulnerability analysis and cybersecurity. These tools are designed to help cybersecurity professionals and analysts identify weaknesses, vulnerabilities, and potential threats within software applications, networks, and systems. While there are various assessment tools available, intermediate-level tools provide a balance between ease of use and advanced functionality. One category of intermediate-level assessment tools includes vulnerability scanners. Vulnerability scanners are automated tools that systematically examine systems, networks, and applications for known vulnerabilities. They compare the characteristics and configurations of scanned systems with a database of known vulnerabilities and provide reports on any identified issues. These tools are invaluable for identifying common vulnerabilities, such as outdated software, misconfigured settings, and missing security patches. One popular intermediate-level vulnerability scanner is Nessus, which offers both free and commercial versions. Nessus provides comprehensive vulnerability scanning capabilities, including scanning for common vulnerabilities and configuration issues. It also offers advanced features like compliance auditing and asset discovery. Another widely used tool is OpenVAS, which is an open-source vulnerability scanner known for its robustness and extensive vulnerability database. Nexpose by Rapid7 is another intermediate-level vulnerability scanner that offers powerful scanning capabilities and risk assessment. Web application scanners are a specialized type of assessment tool designed to identify vulnerabilities specific to web applications and websites. They simulate attacks on web applications to discover security weaknesses, such as SQL injection, cross-site scripting (XSS), and security misconfigurations. Burp Suite, a popular web application security testing tool, falls into the intermediate category. Burp Suite allows security professionals to intercept, manipulate, and analyze web traffic and applications. It includes features for both automated scanning and manual testing. Another tool in this category is Acunetix, known for its comprehensive web vulnerability scanning and robust reporting capabilities. Intermediate-level network assessment tools are essential for evaluating the security of network infrastructure. These tools help identify vulnerabilities in network devices, such as routers, switches, and firewalls, as well as potential security weaknesses in network configurations. One notable tool is Nmap (Network Mapper), which is a versatile and powerful open-source network scanning tool. Nmap can discover hosts, services, and open ports, making it useful for both reconnaissance and vulnerability assessment. It can also detect operating systems and version information. Wireshark is another intermediate-level tool often used for network analysis. It allows users to capture and analyze network packets, helping identify anomalies, security issues, and potential threats. Furthermore, intermediate-level assessment tools for operating system and software security are essential for identifying vulnerabilities within the software stack. These tools focus on assessing the security of operating systems, databases, and application servers. QualysGuard is an intermediate-level tool that provides vulnerability assessment and management services, covering a wide range of software and infrastructure. It offers features such as asset management, policy compliance, and reporting. Retina Network Security Scanner is another tool known for its ability to scan a variety of platforms and applications for vulnerabilities. Database assessment tools are critical for identifying vulnerabilities within databases and database management systems (DBMS). These tools help detect weaknesses that could be exploited by attackers to compromise sensitive data. AppDetectivePRO, an intermediate-level tool, specializes in database security assessments and can identify vulnerabilities, configuration errors, and access control issues within databases. GreenSQL is another tool focused on database security, offering database firewall capabilities and vulnerability scanning. Intermediate-level assessment tools also play a role in cloud security. As organizations increasingly adopt cloud infrastructure and services, assessing the security of cloud-based environments becomes crucial. Tools like CloudSploit and ScoutSuite offer intermediate-level capabilities for auditing and assessing cloud security configurations. These tools help organizations identify misconfigurations, insecure settings, and potential vulnerabilities in their cloud infrastructure. When it comes to mobile application security, intermediate-level assessment tools cater to the unique challenges of mobile app security testing. MobSF (Mobile Security Framework) is an open-source tool that offers dynamic and static analysis of Android and iOS applications. It helps identify vulnerabilities such as insecure storage, data leakage, and insecure communication. Additionally, intermediate-level assessment tools often provide features for generating comprehensive reports. These reports are vital for communicating assessment findings to stakeholders, including system administrators, developers, and executives. Reports typically include detailed information about identified vulnerabilities, their severity, and recommendations for remediation. By using intermediate-level assessment tools, cybersecurity professionals can efficiently identify and prioritize vulnerabilities, reducing the risk of security breaches and data compromises. These tools are versatile and adaptable, making them valuable assets in the ongoing effort to protect systems and data from evolving threats. Furthermore, organizations that implement a robust vulnerability assessment program with intermediate-level tools can demonstrate a commitment to proactive security and compliance with industry standards and regulations. In summary, leveraging intermediate-level assessment tools is a crucial part of vulnerability analysis and cybersecurity. These tools encompass vulnerability scanners, web application scanners, network assessment tools, operating system and software security tools, database assessment tools, cloud security assessment tools, and mobile application security assessment tools. They help identify vulnerabilities, misconfigurations, and security weaknesses across various components of an organization's infrastructure. Effective use of these tools, combined with thorough reporting and remediation efforts, enhances an organization's security posture and reduces the risk of security incidents. Maximizing the potential of vulnerability scanning software is essential for maintaining a robust cybersecurity posture. Vulnerability scanning software plays a crucial role in identifying security weaknesses, misconfigurations, and potential threats within an organization's network, systems, and applications. To harness its full capabilities, organizations need to adopt a proactive and strategic approach to vulnerability management. One key aspect of maximizing the potential of vulnerability scanning software is regular and comprehensive scanning. Organizations should establish a schedule for scanning their entire infrastructure, including both internal and external networks. Regular scans help ensure that newly discovered vulnerabilities are promptly identified and addressed. Furthermore, organizations should configure vulnerability scanning tools to scan all systems, devices, and applications, including those in remote or less-visible parts of the network. In addition to regular scans, organizations should perform scans whenever significant changes are made to the network or when new assets are introduced. This proactive approach helps detect vulnerabilities that may arise due to changes in the environment. Another crucial aspect is defining scanning policies and criteria. Organizations should establish clear policies that govern the frequency and scope of vulnerability scans. These policies should consider factors such as the criticality of systems, the sensitivity of data, and compliance requirements. By defining scanning criteria, organizations can ensure that scans are aligned with their security objectives and priorities. Additionally, organizations should configure scanning tools to use authenticated scans whenever possible. Authenticated scans provide deeper insights into the security posture of systems by allowing the scanner to log in and assess the system from an insider's perspective. This type of scan can identify vulnerabilities that may not be visible from an external perspective, such as missing patches and configuration issues. Vulnerability scanning tools often provide the option to perform authenticated scans using credentials with limited privileges, minimizing the impact on the scanned systems. To maximize the potential of vulnerability scanning software, organizations should establish a workflow for vulnerability remediation. Once vulnerabilities are identified, they need to be prioritized and assigned to the appropriate teams or individuals for resolution. Organizations should define clear roles and responsibilities for addressing vulnerabilities and establish timelines for remediation. Vulnerability scanning tools typically provide severity ratings for identified vulnerabilities, helping organizations prioritize them based on the potential impact on the organization's security. Furthermore, organizations should integrate vulnerability scanning into their change management process. Before implementing changes or updates to systems, applications, or configurations, a vulnerability scan should be conducted to ensure that the changes do not introduce new vulnerabilities or weaken security. Integration with change management helps prevent vulnerabilities from being introduced inadvertently during system changes. Maximizing the potential of vulnerability scanning software also involves leveraging automation and integration capabilities. Vulnerability scanning tools often offer automation features, such as scheduling scans, sending notifications, and generating reports. Organizations should utilize these features to streamline the scanning process and reduce manual effort. Integration with other security tools and systems, such as security information and event management (SIEM) systems and ticketing systems, is essential. Integration allows for the automatic sharing of scan results, alerts, and remediation tickets across the organization's security infrastructure. This integration enables faster response times and a more coordinated approach to vulnerability management. Effective reporting and communication are key to maximizing the potential of vulnerability scanning software. Organizations should generate clear and concise reports that provide actionable insights to both technical and non-technical stakeholders. These reports should include detailed information about identified vulnerabilities, their severity, potential impacts, and recommended remediation steps. Reports should be tailored to the specific needs of different stakeholders, such as IT administrators, security teams, and executives. Additionally, organizations should establish a process for regular communication with stakeholders to ensure that they are informed about the organization's vulnerability management efforts. Furthermore, organizations should invest in training and skill development for their cybersecurity teams. Maximizing the potential of vulnerability scanning software requires expertise in using these tools effectively. Training helps cybersecurity professionals become proficient in configuring, operating, and interpreting scan results. It also keeps them up-to-date with the latest trends and techniques in vulnerability management. Organizations can leverage training resources provided by the vendors of vulnerability scanning software or seek external training and certifications. Finally, organizations should continuously evaluate and evolve their vulnerability management program. The threat landscape is constantly changing, and new vulnerabilities are discovered regularly. Organizations should adapt their scanning practices and strategies to address emerging threats. This may involve adjusting scanning criteria, incorporating threat intelligence feeds, and staying informed about new vulnerability disclosures. In summary, maximizing the potential of vulnerability scanning software is crucial for maintaining a strong cybersecurity posture. To achieve this, organizations should establish regular and comprehensive scanning practices, define clear scanning policies and criteria, use authenticated scans when possible, establish a workflow for remediation, integrate scanning with change management, leverage automation and integration capabilities, prioritize effective reporting and communication, invest in training and skill development, and continuously evaluate and adapt their vulnerability management program. By following these principles, organizations can effectively identify and address vulnerabilities, reducing the risk of security incidents and data breaches.

Chapter 6: Advanced Vulnerability Reporting and Communication

Effective vulnerability reporting techniques are vital in the cybersecurity landscape, as they play a crucial role in ensuring that identified vulnerabilities are addressed promptly and appropriately. Reporting vulnerabilities is a fundamental step in the responsible disclosure process, which aims to minimize the risk of exploitation by malicious actors while allowing organizations to remediate security flaws. One of the first considerations in effective vulnerability reporting is the choice of the appropriate channel. Security researchers, ethical hackers, and concerned individuals should identify the most suitable method for reporting vulnerabilities to the affected organizations. Common reporting channels include dedicated security email addresses, web forms, and third-party platforms like HackerOne and Bugcrowd. Selecting the right channel ensures that the vulnerability report reaches the organization's security team in a timely manner. When preparing a vulnerability report, it is essential to provide clear and concise information about the identified vulnerability. The report should include a detailed description of the vulnerability, its potential impact, and the steps taken to reproduce it. Including proof-of-concept code or examples can significantly assist the organization's security team in understanding the issue and verifying its validity. Additionally, vulnerability reporters should provide information about the environment and configurations in which the vulnerability was discovered. This context can help the organization assess the risk accurately and prioritize remediation efforts. Effectiveness in vulnerability reporting also requires providing recommendations or suggestions for remediation. Vulnerability reporters can propose mitigation strategies or fixes to assist the organization in resolving the issue. While it is not always expected, providing potential solutions demonstrates a proactive approach to helping the organization address the vulnerability. Another essential aspect of effective vulnerability reporting is adherence to responsible disclosure practices. Responsible disclosure emphasizes collaboration between the vulnerability reporter and the organization to mitigate risks. This involves giving the organization a reasonable amount of time to investigate, validate, and remediate the vulnerability before making it public. The exact timeline may vary depending on the severity of the vulnerability and the organization's ability to address it. Maintaining open lines of communication is vital during the responsible disclosure process. Vulnerability reporters should be prepared to answer questions from the organization's security team and provide additional information as needed. Effective communication helps resolve any misunderstandings and ensures a smooth and efficient remediation process. When reporting vulnerabilities, it is essential to consider the sensitivity of the information being disclosed. In some cases, the vulnerability may be tied to sensitive data or confidential systems. Vulnerability reporters should handle such information with care and ensure that it is shared only with the appropriate parties within the organization. This approach helps maintain trust and confidentiality during the reporting process. To enhance the effectiveness of vulnerability reporting, individuals and organizations should also be aware of legal and ethical considerations. Some countries and regions have specific laws and regulations related to the reporting of security vulnerabilities. Understanding the legal landscape and adhering to relevant regulations is essential to avoid unintended legal consequences. Ethical considerations also play a crucial role in vulnerability reporting. Reporters should act responsibly, avoid malicious activities, and prioritize the safety and security of affected systems and data. Responsible disclosure is grounded in ethical behavior, emphasizing the responsible handling of vulnerabilities for the greater good of cybersecurity. Furthermore, organizations can play a significant role in fostering effective vulnerability reporting by establishing clear and accessible reporting mechanisms. They should maintain dedicated email addresses or web forms for receiving vulnerability reports and ensure that these channels are actively monitored. Organizations can also offer guidance on their websites or security pages, outlining the preferred reporting process and expectations for vulnerability reporters. In addition, organizations should commit to timely and transparent communication with reporters throughout the remediation process. Acknowledging receipt of a vulnerability report and providing updates on the progress of remediation can build trust and cooperation. Recognizing the contributions of vulnerability reporters, whether through public acknowledgments or bug bounty programs, is another way organizations can encourage responsible reporting. These acknowledgments serve as positive reinforcement for ethical behavior and can attract more security researchers to help identify vulnerabilities. In summary, effective vulnerability reporting techniques are essential for maintaining a secure digital ecosystem. Vulnerability reporters should choose the appropriate reporting channel, provide clear and concise information, offer recommendations for remediation, adhere to responsible disclosure practices, maintain open communication, handle sensitive information responsibly, consider legal and ethical considerations, and act in a manner that prioritizes cybersecurity and ethical behavior. Organizations, on the other hand, should establish accessible reporting mechanisms, provide guidance to reporters, commit to transparent communication, and recognize the contributions of ethical hackers and security researchers. By working together, reporters and organizations can help identify and address vulnerabilities, ultimately enhancing the overall security of digital systems and applications. Communicating vulnerabilities to stakeholders is a critical aspect of cybersecurity that ensures everyone involved is informed and can take appropriate action. Stakeholders in the context of cybersecurity can encompass a wide range of individuals and groups, including executives, IT teams, developers, third-party vendors, and even customers. Effective communication of vulnerabilities is essential to address security risks, make informed decisions, and protect an organization's reputation. One of the first steps in communicating vulnerabilities is to define a clear and structured process for reporting and disclosure. This process should outline how vulnerabilities are reported, how they are assessed, and how information is disseminated to various stakeholders. Having a well-defined process ensures consistency and reduces confusion when handling different types of vulnerabilities. Transparency is key in vulnerability communication, and organizations should strive to keep stakeholders informed about the progress of vulnerability assessments and remediation efforts. When a vulnerability is identified, the organization's security team should promptly acknowledge receipt of the report and begin the validation process. Timely acknowledgment reassures the reporter that their findings are taken seriously. Next, the security team should conduct a thorough assessment of the vulnerability, evaluating its severity, potential impact, and any potential mitigations. Stakeholders should be kept informed at each stage of this assessment, allowing them to understand the risks and potential consequences associated with the vulnerability. Once the assessment is complete, the organization should establish a remediation plan. The plan should include a timeline for addressing the vulnerability, prioritizing based on severity and potential impact. Stakeholders need to be informed about the remediation plan, including when the vulnerability is expected to be resolved. Transparency regarding timelines helps stakeholders manage their expectations and make informed decisions about their own actions. When it comes to communication, clarity and simplicity are paramount. Technical details about the vulnerability should be communicated in a manner that is understandable to non-technical stakeholders. Plain language explanations can help executives and business leaders grasp the significance of the vulnerability without delving into technical jargon. Conversely, IT and security teams may require more technical details to assess the vulnerability's impact and plan remediation strategies effectively. In addition to communicating with internal stakeholders, organizations should consider external communication when necessary. In some cases, vulnerabilities may have implications for customers or the broader public. In such instances, organizations should have a prepared external communication plan in place. This plan should outline how and when to communicate with affected parties, what information to share, and the steps they should take to protect themselves. Effective external communication can help mitigate the potential fallout from a vulnerability and maintain trust with customers and partners. Vulnerability communication should be a two-way process, and organizations should be receptive to feedback and questions from stakeholders. Stakeholders may have concerns or seek clarification about the vulnerability and its implications. Providing channels for open dialogue and addressing questions promptly fosters trust and collaboration. Moreover, organizations can leverage bug bounty programs to encourage ethical hackers and security researchers to report vulnerabilities. These programs incentivize responsible disclosure and create a positive channel for vulnerability communication. Acknowledging the contributions of these individuals through public recognition or financial rewards can further motivate them to report vulnerabilities responsibly. As part of effective vulnerability communication, organizations should consider categorizing vulnerabilities based on their severity and impact. Common classification systems include the Common Vulnerability Scoring System (CVSS) and the Common Weakness Enumeration (CWE). By categorizing vulnerabilities, organizations can prioritize their response efforts and allocate resources effectively. This helps stakeholders understand the relative importance of different vulnerabilities and guides their decision-making. Organizations should also consider creating and maintaining a vulnerability disclosure policy. This policy outlines the organization's approach to responsible disclosure, including how vulnerabilities are reported, assessed, and communicated. Having a well-documented policy provides clarity for both internal and external stakeholders and sets expectations for responsible disclosure. Furthermore, organizations should conduct regular security awareness training for their employees. This training helps all members of the organization understand their role in identifying and reporting potential vulnerabilities. Employees who are aware of the importance of security are more likely to report suspicious activities or vulnerabilities promptly. In summary, communicating vulnerabilities to stakeholders is a crucial element of effective cybersecurity management. Organizations should establish clear and transparent processes for reporting, assessing, and remediating vulnerabilities. They should prioritize communication clarity and simplicity, both for internal and external stakeholders. Two-way communication channels should be maintained to address questions and concerns. Bug bounty programs can incentivize responsible disclosure, and classification systems help prioritize responses. Vulnerability disclosure policies and security awareness training contribute to a robust vulnerability communication strategy. By embracing these practices, organizations can enhance their cybersecurity posture and maintain trust with their stakeholders.

Chapter 7: Intermediate-Level Remediation Strategies

Developing intermediate remediation plans is a critical phase in the vulnerability management process. Once vulnerabilities have been identified and assessed, organizations need to create effective plans to address them. Intermediate remediation plans are designed to tackle vulnerabilities that fall between the lower-priority issues addressed in routine maintenance and the high-priority vulnerabilities that require immediate attention. These plans bridge the gap, ensuring that security weaknesses are addressed in a timely and systematic manner. The first step in developing an intermediate remediation plan is to prioritize vulnerabilities. Organizations should use risk-based criteria, such as the Common Vulnerability Scoring System (CVSS) scores, to determine the severity and potential impact of each vulnerability. This prioritization helps organizations focus their efforts on the most critical vulnerabilities that pose the greatest risk to their environment. Vulnerabilities that are categorized as moderate or significant in terms of risk may be suitable candidates for intermediate remediation plans. Once vulnerabilities are prioritized, organizations should assemble a dedicated team responsible for addressing them. This team should consist of experts in cybersecurity, system administrators, and relevant application owners. Collaboration between these team members is crucial to develop effective remediation strategies. Next, organizations should establish clear objectives and goals for their intermediate remediation plans. These objectives should outline what the organization aims to achieve through remediation efforts, such as reducing the attack surface, enhancing security posture, or achieving compliance with industry standards. Having well-defined objectives ensures that everyone involved understands the purpose and scope of the remediation efforts. With objectives in place, organizations should perform a detailed analysis of each prioritized vulnerability. This analysis should include an assessment of the affected systems, potential impact, available mitigations, and the effort required to remediate the vulnerability. Understanding these factors helps organizations make informed decisions about the sequence and approach to remediation. Intermediate remediation plans should also incorporate a timeline for addressing vulnerabilities. While high-severity vulnerabilities require immediate attention, intermediate vulnerabilities can be scheduled for remediation based on their risk and available resources. The timeline should outline when each vulnerability is expected to be addressed, taking into account the effort required and the availability of patches or fixes. It's essential to be realistic about timelines to ensure that remediation efforts can be completed effectively. Organizations should consider using a phased approach to intermediate remediation. Rather than attempting to address all vulnerabilities simultaneously, they can group them into manageable phases based on their priority and dependencies. Each phase should have a specific set of vulnerabilities to address, with clearly defined objectives and timelines. This phased approach allows organizations to make steady progress in reducing their vulnerability exposure. Furthermore, organizations should allocate resources and budget for intermediate remediation efforts. These resources may include personnel, tools, and technology required to remediate vulnerabilities. Having a dedicated budget ensures that organizations can invest in the necessary resources to address vulnerabilities effectively. Communication is a key component of intermediate remediation plans. Organizations should maintain open lines of communication with stakeholders, including the executive team, IT staff, and application owners. Stakeholders should be informed about the progress of remediation efforts, any challenges encountered, and the expected outcomes. Regular updates and reporting help maintain transparency and alignment with organizational goals. Intermediate remediation plans should also incorporate a testing and validation phase. Before deploying patches or fixes, organizations should test them in a controlled environment to ensure they do not introduce new issues or disrupt existing systems. Thorough testing helps mitigate the risk of unintended consequences during the remediation process. Additionally, organizations should document their remediation efforts thoroughly. This documentation includes details about each vulnerability, the actions taken to address it, and any associated findings or challenges. Well-documented remediation efforts provide a historical record and serve as a valuable reference for future security assessments. Finally, organizations should conduct a post-remediation assessment to validate the effectiveness of their efforts. This assessment should verify that vulnerabilities have been successfully remediated and that the organization's security posture has improved. Any remaining issues or unexpected outcomes should be addressed promptly. In summary, developing intermediate remediation plans is a crucial step in managing vulnerabilities effectively. These plans help organizations address moderate and significant vulnerabilities in a structured and prioritized manner. Key elements of effective intermediate remediation plans include prioritization, team collaboration, clear objectives, detailed analysis, realistic timelines, phased approaches, resource allocation, communication, testing, documentation, and post-remediation assessments. By following these principles, organizations can reduce their vulnerability exposure and enhance their overall cybersecurity posture.

Implementing remediation strategies effectively is a critical component of cybersecurity management. Once vulnerabilities have been identified and assessed, organizations must take decisive action to address them. The goal of remediation is to reduce or eliminate security risks and protect the organization's digital assets. Effective implementation of remediation strategies involves a systematic and well-planned approach. The first step in this process is to prioritize vulnerabilities based on their severity and potential impact. Not all vulnerabilities are created equal, and organizations need to focus their resources on addressing the most critical ones. Prioritization criteria, such as the Common Vulnerability Scoring System (CVSS) scores, can help organizations determine which vulnerabilities require immediate attention. Once vulnerabilities are prioritized, organizations should assemble a dedicated remediation team. This team should consist of experts in cybersecurity, system administrators, and application owners. Collaboration among team members is crucial to developing and executing effective remediation strategies. Before implementing remediation measures, organizations need to establish clear objectives and goals. These objectives should outline what the organization aims to achieve through remediation, whether it's reducing the attack surface, enhancing security posture, or achieving compliance with industry standards. Having well-defined objectives ensures that everyone involved understands the purpose and scope of the remediation efforts. With objectives in place, organizations should analyze each prioritized vulnerability in detail. This analysis should include an assessment of the affected systems, potential impact, available mitigations, and the effort required to remediate the vulnerability. Understanding these factors helps organizations make informed decisions about the sequence and approach to remediation. Effective remediation strategies also require the development of a comprehensive remediation plan. The plan should outline the specific steps and actions required to address each vulnerability. It should include timelines, resource allocation, and responsibilities for each task. A well-structured remediation plan ensures that remediation efforts are organized, efficient, and trackable. Testing and validation are critical components of effective remediation. Before deploying patches or fixes, organizations should thoroughly test them in a controlled environment. Testing helps ensure that the remediation measures do not introduce new issues or disrupt existing systems. Any identified issues should be addressed promptly before proceeding with the remediation. Communication is key throughout the remediation process. Organizations should maintain open lines of communication with stakeholders, including the executive team, IT staff, and application owners. Stakeholders should be informed about the progress of remediation efforts, any challenges encountered, and the expected outcomes. Regular updates and reporting help maintain transparency and alignment with organizational goals. Resource allocation is another critical aspect of effective remediation. Organizations should allocate the necessary resources, including personnel, tools, and technology, to support the remediation efforts. Having dedicated resources ensures that remediation tasks can be completed effectively and within the established timelines. Documentation is essential to track and record all remediation activities. Organizations should maintain detailed records of each vulnerability, the actions taken to address it, and any associated findings or challenges. Well-documented remediation efforts provide a historical record and serve as a valuable reference for future security assessments. In addition to documentation, organizations should conduct a post-remediation assessment to validate the effectiveness of their efforts. This assessment should verify that vulnerabilities have been successfully remediated and that the organization's security posture has improved. Any remaining issues or unexpected outcomes should be addressed promptly. Furthermore, organizations should consider leveraging automation and security tools to streamline and enhance their remediation efforts. Automation can help identify vulnerabilities, apply patches, and perform routine security tasks more efficiently. Finally, ongoing monitoring and continuous improvement are essential for maintaining the effectiveness of remediation strategies. The threat landscape is constantly evolving, and new vulnerabilities emerge regularly. Organizations should stay vigilant, monitor their systems for vulnerabilities, and adapt their remediation strategies accordingly. In summary, implementing remediation strategies effectively is crucial for managing cybersecurity risks and protecting an organization's digital assets. Key elements of effective remediation include prioritization, team collaboration, clear objectives, detailed analysis, structured remediation plans, testing, communication, resource allocation, documentation, post-remediation assessment, automation, and continuous improvement. By following these principles, organizations can reduce security risks, enhance their cybersecurity posture, and respond effectively to emerging threats.

Chapter 8: Security Practices for Intermediate Analysts

Intermediate-level security protocols and best practices are essential components of a robust cybersecurity strategy. As organizations continue to navigate the complex landscape of digital threats, it becomes increasingly important to implement security measures that go beyond the basics. Intermediate-level security protocols are designed to provide enhanced protection and resilience against a wide range of cyberattacks. One of the foundational elements of intermediate-level security is the implementation of network segmentation. Network segmentation involves dividing an organization's network into separate segments or zones, each with its own security controls and access restrictions. This practice helps contain potential breaches, limiting the lateral movement of attackers within the network. By segmenting the network, organizations can isolate critical systems and data, reducing the risk of a widespread compromise. In addition to network segmentation, the use of intrusion detection and prevention systems (IDPS) is crucial at the intermediate level. IDPS solutions are designed to monitor network traffic for suspicious or malicious activities and take action to block or mitigate threats in real-time. These systems provide organizations with an additional layer of defense against known and emerging threats. Regularly updating and patching systems and software is a fundamental best practice at any security level, but it becomes even more critical at the intermediate level. Intermediate-level security protocols should include a well-defined patch management process that ensures timely updates to operating systems, applications, and firmware. Unpatched vulnerabilities can be exploited by attackers, making regular updates a top priority. Access control and authentication mechanisms also play a central role in intermediate-level security. Organizations should implement strong authentication methods, such as multi-factor authentication (MFA), to verify the identity of users and devices. MFA adds an extra layer of security by requiring users to provide multiple forms of authentication, such as a password and a fingerprint or a smart card. Effective access control ensures that only authorized individuals have access to sensitive data and systems. Furthermore, organizations should establish role-based access control (RBAC) policies to limit user privileges based on their specific job roles. This practice minimizes the risk of unauthorized access and helps contain potential breaches. Intermediate-level security protocols should also address the monitoring and logging of security events. Implementing a Security Information and Event Management (SIEM) system is a best practice for collecting, correlating, and analyzing security-related data from various sources. SIEM solutions enable organizations to detect and respond to security incidents more effectively by providing real-time insights into network activities. Alongside SIEM, organizations should establish a Security Operations Center (SOC) or a Managed Security Service Provider

(MSSP) to monitor and respond to security incidents around the clock. A SOC or MSSP enhances an organization's ability to detect and mitigate threats promptly. Encryption is a vital component of intermediate-level security. Organizations should encrypt sensitive data both at rest and in transit to protect it from unauthorized access. Transport Layer Security (TLS) and Secure Sockets Layer (SSL) are commonly used protocols for securing data in transit. For data at rest, encryption solutions such as full-disk encryption or file-level encryption should be implemented. Regular vulnerability assessments and penetration testing are essential best practices at the intermediate security level. Vulnerability assessments involve scanning systems and applications for known vulnerabilities and weaknesses. Penetration testing goes a step further, simulating real-world attacks to identify potential vulnerabilities that may not be detected by automated tools. Both practices help organizations proactively address security weaknesses. Employee training and awareness are critical for the success of intermediate-level security protocols. Employees should receive ongoing cybersecurity training to recognize phishing attempts, social engineering tactics, and other common attack vectors. Educated and vigilant employees can act as an additional line of defense against cyber threats. Another important aspect of intermediate-level security is incident response planning. Organizations should develop and regularly test incident response plans to ensure they are well-prepared to handle security incidents effectively. A robust incident response plan outlines the steps to take when a breach is detected, including communication, containment, eradication, and recovery procedures. Finally, organizations should stay informed about emerging threats and industry best practices. Participating in information sharing and threat intelligence communities can provide valuable insights into new attack techniques and vulnerabilities. Regularly updating security policies and procedures to align with the evolving threat landscape is essential. In summary, intermediate-level security protocols and best practices are indispensable for organizations seeking to enhance their cybersecurity posture. These measures, including network segmentation, intrusion detection and prevention, patch management, strong authentication, access control, monitoring, encryption, vulnerability assessments, employee training, incident response planning, and staying informed, collectively contribute to a robust security strategy. By implementing these intermediate-level security measures, organizations can better defend against a wide range of cyber threats and safeguard their digital assets.

Collaboration is a fundamental aspect of successful vulnerability mitigation efforts. In today's interconnected digital landscape, organizations face a multitude of cyber threats that require collective action to combat effectively. Working collaboratively with various stakeholders, both within and outside the organization, can significantly enhance the ability to identify, assess, and remediate vulnerabilities. One of the key aspects of collaborative vulnerability mitigation is establishing clear communication channels. Organizations should have well-defined lines of communication to share information about vulnerabilities, threats, and mitigation strategies. Effective communication ensures that all relevant parties are informed and can act swiftly when necessary. Internal collaboration is critical within an organization. Different departments, such as IT, security, and development, should work together seamlessly to address vulnerabilities. This collaboration helps bridge gaps in understanding and ensures that all teams are aligned in their efforts to protect the organization's assets. Collaborative vulnerability mitigation extends beyond an organization's boundaries. Collaboration with vendors and third-party partners is essential, as vulnerabilities can exist in software and systems provided by external parties. Organizations should have processes in place to engage with vendors and receive timely updates and patches to address vulnerabilities. Moreover, collaborating with industry peers through information sharing and threat intelligence communities can provide valuable insights into emerging threats and vulnerabilities. These communities allow organizations to stay ahead of cyber threats by learning from the experiences of others. Government agencies and cybersecurity organizations also play a vital role in collaborative vulnerability mitigation efforts. Many countries have established Computer Emergency Response Teams (CERTs) or similar entities to facilitate information sharing and coordination during cybersecurity incidents. Collaborating with these agencies can help organizations access resources and expertise needed to respond effectively to vulnerabilities and cyberattacks. Collaborative vulnerability mitigation is not limited to addressing known vulnerabilities but also involves proactive efforts to discover and address security weaknesses. Organizations can engage in bug bounty programs, where ethical hackers and security researchers are incentivized to identify vulnerabilities in exchange for rewards. These programs harness the collective expertise of the cybersecurity community to find and fix vulnerabilities before malicious actors exploit them. Cross-functional teams within organizations, often referred to as vulnerability assessment teams, are crucial for effective collaboration. These teams bring together individuals with diverse skills and expertise, including security analysts, system administrators, and application developers. Their collective knowledge and experience enable organizations to comprehensively assess vulnerabilities from various angles. Collaborative vulnerability mitigation efforts should prioritize vulnerability management processes. Vulnerability management encompasses the entire lifecycle of identifying, assessing, prioritizing, mitigating, and monitoring vulnerabilities. Regularly scheduled vulnerability scans and assessments are essential components of this process. These activities provide organizations with visibility into their security posture and help identify vulnerabilities that need attention.

Once vulnerabilities are identified, they should be assessed and prioritized based on factors like their potential impact and exploitability. Collaborative decision-making processes should be in place to determine which vulnerabilities require immediate action and which can be addressed over time. Collaboration extends to the remediation phase as well. Teams responsible for patching systems, applying security updates, or implementing code changes should work closely to ensure that vulnerabilities are effectively addressed. Security teams should collaborate with system administrators and developers to coordinate the deployment of patches and fixes without disrupting critical business operations. Regular communication and progress tracking are essential throughout the mitigation process to keep all stakeholders informed. Effective collaboration also includes establishing incident response procedures. In the event of a security incident related to a vulnerability, a well-prepared incident response team should be able to coordinate and execute a swift and efficient response. Collaboration within this team, consisting of security experts, legal counsel, public relations, and IT staff, is essential to mitigate the impact of the incident. Furthermore, collaboration can extend to external security vendors and experts who may assist in analyzing and containing the incident. Continuous monitoring and feedback loops are vital for improving collaborative vulnerability mitigation efforts. After vulnerabilities are mitigated, organizations should conduct post-incident reviews to identify lessons learned and areas for improvement. Feedback from all stakeholders, including internal teams and external partners, can inform adjustments to vulnerability management processes. Ultimately, working collaboratively in vulnerability mitigation efforts enhances an organization's ability to defend against cyber threats. Effective communication, internal and external collaboration, cross-functional teams, proactive vulnerability discovery, vulnerability management processes, incident response procedures, and feedback mechanisms all contribute to a comprehensive and robust approach to cybersecurity. By fostering a culture of collaboration, organizations can better protect their assets and respond effectively to the ever-evolving threat landscape.

Chapter 9: Collaborative Approaches to Vulnerability Mitigation

Achieving proficiency in intermediate vulnerability analysis is a critical milestone for cybersecurity professionals. At this level, individuals have already gained foundational knowledge and experience in identifying and assessing vulnerabilities. Now, they are ready to dive deeper into the intricacies of vulnerability analysis to enhance their skills and contribute more effectively to an organization's security posture. Intermediate vulnerability analysts build upon their understanding of the software landscape, common types of vulnerabilities, and the role of zero-day exploits. They have the ability to identify vulnerabilities in code, but they seek to refine their techniques and broaden their knowledge. One key aspect of achieving proficiency in intermediate vulnerability analysis is mastering vulnerability scanning tools. These tools are essential for automating the process of identifying vulnerabilities in systems and applications. Intermediate analysts should be well-versed in the operation of various scanning tools and understand their strengths and limitations. They learn to configure scans, interpret scan results, and prioritize vulnerabilities based on their severity and potential impact. Furthermore, intermediate analysts become proficient in reporting and documenting vulnerabilities. Effective communication of vulnerabilities to relevant stakeholders is crucial for timely remediation. They create detailed reports that provide a clear picture of the vulnerabilities, their potential impact, and recommended remediation steps. These reports are valuable for system administrators, developers, and security teams as they work together to address vulnerabilities. Remediation strategies for novices are often straightforward, focusing on applying patches and updates. However, achieving proficiency at the intermediate level involves developing more nuanced remediation strategies. Intermediate analysts explore various remediation techniques, including code changes, configuration adjustments, and the deployment of security controls. They understand the importance of balancing security requirements with business needs to ensure that remediation efforts are effective without causing unnecessary disruptions. Best practices in software security are another area of focus for those seeking proficiency in intermediate vulnerability analysis. Intermediate analysts delve into security principles and methodologies that help prevent vulnerabilities from arising in the first place. They learn about secure coding practices, security architecture, and secure development lifecycles. By understanding how to build secure software, they can contribute to reducing the prevalence of vulnerabilities. To become proficient, intermediate analysts must also develop expertise in vulnerability assessment and analysis tools. These tools go beyond simple scanning and require a deeper understanding of vulnerabilities and their potential impact. Intermediate analysts use these tools to conduct in-depth assessments, identify false positives, and validate vulnerabilities. Becoming a novice vulnerability analyst is an achievement in itself, but reaching proficiency at the intermediate level takes dedication and continuous learning. Intermediate analysts should actively seek opportunities for professional development, such as attending security conferences, participating in capture the flag (CTF) competitions, and pursuing relevant certifications. These activities allow them to stay current with the evolving threat landscape and hone their skills. Additionally, joining cybersecurity communities and forums provides a platform for sharing knowledge and learning from peers. Collaborating with experienced professionals and exchanging insights is invaluable for growth. As intermediate vulnerability analysts advance in their careers, they may also specialize in specific areas of vulnerability analysis, such as web application security, network security, or mobile application security. Specialization allows them to deepen their expertise and become subject matter experts in their chosen field. Furthermore, achieving proficiency at the intermediate level opens up opportunities for leadership roles within cybersecurity teams. Intermediate analysts can take on mentoring roles, guiding novice analysts, and contributing to the development of organizational security strategies. Their proficiency in vulnerability analysis makes them valuable assets to organizations seeking to strengthen their cybersecurity defenses. In summary, achieving proficiency in intermediate vulnerability analysis is a significant step in a cybersecurity professional's journey.

It involves mastering vulnerability scanning tools, effective reporting and documentation, nuanced remediation strategies, best practices in software security, expertise in assessment and analysis tools, and a commitment to ongoing learning and specialization. Intermediate analysts play a vital role in identifying and mitigating vulnerabilities, contributing to a more secure digital landscape. Their expertise is invaluable in defending against the ever-evolving threat landscape, and their dedication to continuous improvement is essential for staying ahead of cyber adversaries.

Chapter 10: Mastering Intermediate-Level Vulnerability Analysis

Advancing your skills as an intermediate analyst is an exciting and rewarding journey in the world of cybersecurity. At this stage of your career, you've already laid a solid foundation in vulnerability analysis and have gained valuable experience. Now, it's time to take your expertise to the next level and become a more proficient and effective cybersecurity professional. One key aspect of advancing your skills is deepening your knowledge of software vulnerabilities. You've already learned about common types of vulnerabilities, but it's essential to go deeper and understand their intricacies. This includes exploring the various attack vectors, exploitation techniques, and potential impacts associated with different types of vulnerabilities. By gaining a more comprehensive understanding of vulnerabilities, you'll be better equipped to identify, assess, and mitigate them effectively. Another critical area for advancement is the development of your analytical skills. As an intermediate analyst, you've honed your ability to identify vulnerabilities in code and systems, but now it's time to refine your analytical thinking. This involves examining vulnerabilities from multiple angles, considering potential attack scenarios, and assessing their significance within the broader context of an organization's security posture. Analytical thinking allows you to prioritize vulnerabilities based on their risk and potential impact, helping organizations allocate resources more effectively. Mastering vulnerability assessment tools is a crucial step in advancing your skills. You've likely used various scanning and assessment tools as a novice and intermediate analyst, but now it's time to become a true expert. This means not only knowing how to operate these tools proficiently but also understanding their inner workings, limitations, and customization options. Being able to fine-tune scanning tools to suit specific needs and interpret their results accurately is a valuable skill. Additionally, you should explore advanced vulnerability assessment tools that provide in-depth insights and help identify complex vulnerabilities that automated scans may miss. Ethical hacking and penetration testing are essential aspects of advancing your skills as an intermediate analyst. While you've already gained experience in identifying vulnerabilities, ethical hacking and penetration testing take your capabilities to a higher level. These activities involve actively simulating attacks on systems and applications to discover vulnerabilities, weaknesses, and potential entry points for adversaries. By stepping into the shoes of a cyber attacker, you'll gain a deeper understanding of the vulnerabilities you're trying to defend against. Furthermore, ethical hacking and penetration testing provide practical experience in exploiting vulnerabilities, which can be invaluable in enhancing your defensive strategies. As you advance, you'll also delve into the world of zero-day vulnerabilities and exploits. Zero-day vulnerabilities are those for which no patch or fix is available, making them highly attractive to attackers. Understanding how these vulnerabilities are discovered, exploited, and ultimately mitigated is a critical skill for an intermediate analyst. You'll learn about responsible disclosure practices, coordination with vendors, and the ethical considerations surrounding zero-day exploits. In addition to technical skills, advancing your skills as an intermediate analyst involves developing strong communication and leadership abilities. Effective communication is essential for conveying the severity and impact of vulnerabilities to stakeholders and decision-makers. You'll refine your report-writing skills, ensuring that your findings are clear, actionable, and persuasive. Moreover, you'll play a more significant role in guiding remediation efforts, collaborating with development teams, and advising on security best practices. Leadership skills come into play as you may take on mentoring roles, providing guidance and support to junior analysts and contributing to the overall growth of your cybersecurity team. Continued professional development is a core element of advancing your skills. Cybersecurity is a rapidly evolving field, with new threats and technologies emerging regularly. As an intermediate analyst, you should actively seek opportunities for learning and growth. This may include pursuing advanced certifications, attending cybersecurity conferences, participating in capture the flag (CTF) competitions, and joining specialized communities or forums. Engaging with the broader cybersecurity community can provide valuable insights and expose you to cutting-edge techniques and practices. Finally, don't underestimate the importance of ethical and legal considerations in your role as an intermediate analyst. You'll be dealing with sensitive information and potentially conducting activities that simulate cyberattacks. Understanding and adhering t

o ethical guidelines, as well as compliance with relevant laws and regulations, is paramount. By advancing your skills as an intermediate analyst, you'll become a more valuable asset to your organization and the broader cybersecurity community. Your enhanced expertise in software vulnerabilities, analytical thinking, assessment tools, ethical hacking, zero-day vulnerabilities, communication, leadership, and ongoing professional development will set you on a path to success in the dynamic and ever-evolving field of cybersecurity. As you continue to grow and excel in your role, you'll contribute to strengthening the defenses against cyber threats and making the digital world a safer place for all.

BOOK 3
MASTERING ZERO DAY
ADVANCED STRATEGIES FOR VULNERABILITY
DISCOVERY AND REMEDIATION

ROB BOTWRIGHT

Chapter 1: Advanced Zero Day Vulnerability Concepts

Exploring complex zero-day scenarios is a captivating and intellectually stimulating journey within the realm of cybersecurity. As an advanced analyst, you have already honed your skills in identifying, analyzing, and mitigating vulnerabilities, but now it's time to dive deep into the most challenging and elusive of them all—the zero-day vulnerability. Zero-day vulnerabilities are a special category of software flaws. They are called "zero-day" because, at the time of discovery, there are zero days of protection available to users. This means that no patch or update exists to fix the vulnerability, leaving systems and applications exposed to potential exploitation. Understanding the intricacies of zero-day vulnerabilities and their associated scenarios is essential for cybersecurity professionals seeking to defend against them. In complex zero-day scenarios, you'll encounter vulnerabilities that are entirely unknown to the software vendor and the cybersecurity community. These vulnerabilities often exist in the hidden depths of software code, waiting to be discovered by cyber adversaries. Your mission is to explore these scenarios, dissect them, and develop effective strategies for mitigating the risks they pose. One key aspect of exploring complex zero-day scenarios is understanding the discovery process. Zero-day vulnerabilities are typically discovered by security researchers, ethical hackers, or cybercriminals. While responsible disclosure is the ethical approach, some vulnerabilities may be exploited before they are reported to vendors and patched. By delving into the discovery process, you'll gain insights into how vulnerabilities are found, the motivations of those who discover them, and the ethical considerations surrounding disclosure. Moreover, you'll learn about the intricacies of coordinating with software vendors and affected organizations to ensure timely patching and protection. Another critical aspect is the anatomy of zero-day exploits. Zero-day vulnerabilities alone do not pose an immediate threat; they become dangerous when they are weaponized into exploits. In complex zero-day scenarios, you'll explore how these exploits are crafted, enabling attackers to take advantage of the vulnerabilities. You'll learn about the techniques and tools used to create zero-day exploits, as well as the factors that determine their success. Understanding the offensive side of zero-day vulnerabilities is essential for effective defense. Complex zero-day scenarios also involve ethical considerations. You'll delve into the ethical dilemmas surrounding the use of zero-day vulnerabilities for offense and defense. Ethical hackers and security researchers play a vital role in discovering and reporting zero-day vulnerabilities, but they also grapple with questions about responsible disclosure and the potential impact of their findings. Balancing the need for transparency and protection is a complex task. Moreover, you'll explore the legal aspects of zero-day vulnerabilities, such as the legality of researching, disclosing, and using zero-day exploits. Cybersecurity professionals must navigate a complex legal landscape while operating within the bounds of the law. In-depth knowledge of these ethical and legal considerations is crucial in complex zero-day scenarios. As an advanced analyst, you'll also explore the world of advanced threat actors and their motivations. Complex zero-day scenarios often involve state-sponsored or highly sophisticated cybercriminal groups. Understanding their tactics, techniques, and procedures (TTPs) is essential for anticipating and defending against zero-day attacks. You'll delve into threat intelligence, tracking emerging threats, and staying ahead of adversaries. Additionally, you'll explore the role of security vendors and their contributions to mitigating zero-day vulnerabilities. Advanced security solutions, such as intrusion detection systems, sandboxes, and threat intelligence platforms, play a critical role in identifying and stopping zero-day attacks. You'll learn how these technologies work and how to integrate them into your organization's security strategy effectively. Furthermore, exploring complex zero-day scenarios involves continuous learning and staying up to date with emerging threats. The cybersecurity landscape is dynamic, with new vulnerabilities and exploits emerging regularly. As an advanced analyst, you'll actively engage in threat research, monitor cybersecurity news, and participate in information-sharing communities. Collaboration with peers and experts in the field is essential for staying informed and adapting to evolving threats. Finally, you'll develop strategies for proactive defense against zero-day vulnerabilities. While it's impossible to predict every zero-day scenario, you can adopt a proactive security posture that reduces the attack surface and minimizes the impact of potential zero-day attacks. This includes implementing robust security policies, conducting regular security assessments, and fostering a culture of cybersecurity within your organization. In summary, exploring complex zero-day scenarios is an advanced and intellectually stimulating aspect of cybersecurity. It involves understanding the discovery process, the anatomy of zero-day exploits, ethical and legal considerations, threat actors and motivations, the role of security vendors, continuous learning, and proactive defense strategies. By mastering these elements, cybersecurity professionals can become adept at defending against the most elusive and challenging vulnerabilities in the digital landscape. Their expertise is essential for safeguarding critical systems and data against zero-day threats, contributing to a more secure and resilient digital world.

Delving into the world of cybersecurity at an advanced level, we embark on a journey to gain an in-depth understanding of advanced vulnerability concepts. As you've progressed through the ranks of novice and intermediate analysts, you've already grasped the fundamentals of vulnerabilities and their associated risks. Now, it's time to explore the nuances and complexities that come with advanced vulnerability concepts. At this stage of your cybersecurity career, you're no longer just identifying and patching vulnerabilities; you're becoming a true expert in the field. One of the first topics to explore is the realm of zero-day vulnerabilities, which we briefly touched upon in the previous chapter. Zero-day vulnerabilities are software flaws that are discovered and exploited by cyber attackers before software vendors even become aware of them. These vulnerabilities are like hidden landmines in the digital landscape, ready to be triggered by malicious actors. Understanding zero-day vulnerabilities requires diving deep into their discovery, exploitation, and mitigation. You'll explore the processes and tools used by security researchers and ethical hackers to uncover these hidden threats. Moreover, you'll gain insights into the responsible disclosure of zero-day vulnerabilities and the ethical considerations surrounding their use. Zero-day vulnerabilities are a constant cat-and-mouse game between attackers and defenders, making them a fascinating subject for advanced study. Next on our journey is the exploration of advanced exploitation techniques. As an advanced cybersecurity professional, you're not just interested in identifying vulnerabilities; you want to understand how they can be exploited. This involves going beyond basic exploitation methods and delving into more sophisticated techniques used by cybercriminals and state-sponsored actors. You'll learn about advanced exploitation frameworks and tools that can be used to compromise systems and applications. By understanding the intricacies of exploitation, you'll be better equipped to defend against these attacks. Ethical considerations play a significant role in advanced vulnerability analysis. You'll explore the ethical dilemmas faced by security researchers and ethical hackers when dealing with zero-day vulnerabilities and exploits. Balancing the need for responsible disclosure with the potential harm of these vulnerabilities in the wrong hands is a complex and challenging task. Moreover, you'll delve into the legal aspects of vulnerability research and disclosure, ensuring that your actions remain within the bounds of the law. Understanding the ethical and legal dimensions of advanced vulnerability concepts is essential for maintaining professional integrity. The advanced analyst's journey also takes us into the realm of offensive and defensive tactics in zero-day exploitation. You'll explore not only how attackers leverage zero-day vulnerabilities but also how defenders can protect against them. This involves gaining insights into intrusion detection and prevention systems, security monitoring, and incident response. You'll learn about the latest threat intelligence techniques and how they can be used to proactively defend against zero-day attacks. Furthermore, you'll delve into the world of penetration testing at an advanced level. Penetration testing goes beyond basic vulnerability scanning and simulates real-world attacks on systems and applications. Advanced penetration testing techniques involve complex attack scenarios, persistence mechanisms, and lateral movement within a target network. You'll become proficient in conducting in-depth penetration tests that provide organizations with a comprehensive assessment of their security posture. Additionally, you'll explore the ethical considerations surrounding penetration testing, ensuring that your activities remain within ethical and legal boundaries. Collaboration and information sharing are vital in the realm of advanced vulnerability concepts. You'll actively engage with the broader cybersecurity community, participating in threat sharing platforms, forums, and collaborative projects. The exchange of knowledge and expertise is crucial for staying ahead of emerging threats and evolving attack techniques. Moreover, you'll explore the world of responsible disclosure programs offered by software vendors and security organizations. These programs facilitate the responsible reporting of vulnerabilities and the coordination of patching efforts. By participating in these programs, you'll contribute to the overall security of the digital ecosystem. Finally, as you gain an in-depth understanding of advanced vulnerability concepts, you'll be prepared to take on leadership roles within your organization. You'll become a mentor and guide for junior analysts, helping them navigate the complexities of cybersecurity. Your expertise will be sought after in strategic decision-making, as you provide insights into risk management and security posture improvement. Your ability to communicate advanced concepts effectively will be instrumental in driving cybersecurity initiatives. In summary, gaining an in-depth understanding of advanced vulnerability concepts is a natural progression for cybersecurity professionals seeking to reach the pinnacle of their field. You'll explore zero-day vulnerabilities, advanced exploitation techniques, ethical and legal considerations, offensive and defensive tactics, penetration testing, collaboration, responsible disclosure, and leadership roles. By mastering these advanced concepts, you'll become a true expert in the world of cybersecurity, contributing to the protection of digital assets and the advancement of the field itself. Your knowledge and expertise will be invaluable in defending against the most sophisticated and elusive cyber threats, making the digital world a safer place for all.

Chapter 2: Deep Dive into Exploitation Techniques

As we delve deeper into the world of cybersecurity and advanced vulnerability analysis, we reach a pivotal point in our journey—expert-level exploitation strategies. At this stage, you've already acquired a wealth of knowledge and experience in identifying, analyzing, and mitigating vulnerabilities. Now, it's time to elevate your skills to the highest level, becoming a true expert in the art of exploitation. Expert-level exploitation strategies are not for the faint of heart; they require a deep understanding of software vulnerabilities, intricate knowledge of system internals, and the ability to think like an adversary. One of the first aspects we'll explore is the anatomy of advanced zero-day exploits. Zero-day exploits are at the forefront of cyber warfare, and understanding how they are constructed is essential for both offense and defense. You'll delve into the inner workings of zero-day exploits, from crafting reliable exploits to bypassing modern security mechanisms. Learning about advanced exploitation frameworks and tools used by both ethical hackers and malicious actors will provide you with the insights needed to defend against sophisticated attacks. Moreover, you'll explore the world of ethical hacking and penetration testing at an expert level. You're no longer just simulating attacks; you're conducting highly sophisticated and stealthy operations that mimic the tactics of real-world adversaries. These advanced penetration tests involve complex attack scenarios, custom malware development, and the use of advanced persistence techniques. Your goal is to provide organizations with a realistic assessment of their security posture, uncovering vulnerabilities that others might miss. Ethical considerations continue to be a crucial part of your journey as an expert-level analyst. You'll navigate the ethical dilemmas faced by those who possess advanced exploitation skills. The responsible disclosure of zero-day vulnerabilities becomes even more critical as your expertise grows. You'll grapple with questions about the potential harm of your findings versus the need for transparency and protection. Balancing these ethical considerations requires a deep sense of responsibility and a commitment to the greater good. Legal aspects of vulnerability research and disclosure also come into sharper focus. You'll explore the legal landscape surrounding advanced exploitation and hacking techniques. Understanding the legal boundaries and potential consequences of your actions is essential to maintaining professional integrity. Moreover, you'll become well-versed in the legal protections offered to security researchers and ethical hackers who act responsibly. Beyond offensive tactics, expert-level exploitation strategies encompass advanced defensive measures. You'll gain insights into the latest intrusion detection and prevention systems, security monitoring, and incident response techniques. Your goal is not only to understand how attackers operate but also to develop robust defensive strategies that thwart their advances. Threat intelligence becomes a powerful tool in your arsenal. You'll learn to gather and analyze intelligence to stay one step ahead of emerging threats. Advanced threat modeling and analysis techniques allow you to anticipate and proactively defend against sophisticated adversaries. Collaboration and information sharing continue to play a vital role in your journey. You'll actively participate in the global cybersecurity community, contributing your expertise and insights to the collective defense against cyber threats. Engaging with peers, attending security conferences, and collaborating on research projects are essential aspects of your professional development. Additionally, you'll explore the world of responsible disclosure programs at an expert level. These programs enable you to work closely with software vendors and security organizations to coordinate the responsible reporting and patching of vulnerabilities. Your expertise in this area contributes to the overall security of the digital ecosystem. As an expert-level analyst, you're also prepared to take on leadership roles within your organization. You become a mentor, guiding junior analysts in navigating the complexities of cybersecurity. Your insights into risk management, security posture improvement, and strategic decision-making are highly sought after. Your ability to communicate complex concepts effectively is instrumental in driving cybersecurity initiatives forward. In summary, expert-level exploitation strategies represent the pinnacle of your journey in the world of advanced vulnerability analysis. You've explored the anatomy of advanced zero-day exploits, advanced penetration testing, ethical and legal considerations, advanced defense tactics, threat intelligence, collaboration, responsible disclosure, and leadership roles. By mastering these expert-level concepts, you've become a true authority in the field of cybersecurity. Your knowledge and expertise are invaluable in defending against the most sophisticated and elusive cyber threats, shaping the future of cybersecurity, and contributing to a safer digital world for all.

Now that you've reached the zenith of your cybersecurity journey, it's time to delve into the most advanced and intricate aspect of the field—mastering advanced exploitation techniques. At this stage, you've accumulated a wealth of knowledge and experience in identifying, analyzing, and mitigating vulnerabilities. You've explored the world of zero-day vulnerabilities, advanced exploitation, ethical considerations, and advanced defense tactics. Now, it's time to ascend to the highest echelons of expertise in the art of exploitation. Mastering advanced exploitation techniques requires a profound understanding of software vulnerabilities, a deep dive into system internals, and the ability to think and act like a true adversary. The first topic we'll explore is the evolution of zero-day exploits. Zero-day vulnerabilities are the most coveted and dangerous vulnerabilities in the cybersecurity landscape. Understanding their evolution is crucial because it gives you insights into how attackers continually adapt and innovate. You'll explore the history of zero-day exploits, from their early days to the most cutting-edge techniques used by state-sponsored actors and cybercriminals. Studying this evolution provides you with a historical perspective on the cat-and-mouse game between attackers and defenders. Advanced exploitation frameworks and tools are at the core of your expertise. You're no longer just using existing tools; you're developing your own advanced exploits and payloads tailored to specific targets. Customization and sophistication are the hallmarks of your work. You'll delve into advanced techniques such as heap spraying, return-oriented programming (ROP), and just-in-time (JIT) exploitation. These techniques allow you to bypass modern security mechanisms and execute arbitrary code with precision. Moreover, you'll explore the world of privilege escalation and persistence. Advanced adversaries aim not only to compromise systems but also to maintain their foothold for as long as possible. You'll master techniques for elevating privileges on compromised systems, such as kernel exploitation and privilege escalation vulnerabilities. Maintaining persistence involves developing stealthy and resilient backdoors that withstand security updates and patches. Your expertise in this area allows you to simulate the tactics used by advanced threat actors. Ethical considerations continue to be paramount in your journey. You'll navigate complex ethical dilemmas as you wield advanced exploitation techniques. The responsible disclosure of zero-day vulnerabilities becomes even more critical as your skills reach new heights. You'll grapple with the potential consequences of your actions and weigh them against the need for transparency and protection. Balancing these ethical considerations requires an unwavering commitment to the greater good. The legal landscape surrounding advanced exploitation and hacking techniques becomes even more intricate. You'll delve into the nuances of cybercrime laws, international regulations, and the legal protections offered to security researchers and ethical hackers. Understanding the legal boundaries and potential repercussions of your actions is essential for maintaining professional integrity. Advanced defensive measures remain a focal point of your expertise. You're not just defending against known threats; you're anticipating and thwarting sophisticated attacks. You'll explore advanced threat intelligence and proactive defense strategies that keep you ahead of emerging threats. Threat modeling and analysis techniques become second nature to you. You'll identify vulnerabilities and weaknesses in systems and applications before adversaries do. This proactive approach to defense is critical in the ever-evolving landscape of cybersecurity. Collaboration and information sharing reach a new level of sophistication. You're actively engaged in the highest levels of the global cybersecurity community. You'll collaborate on cutting-edge research projects, share threat intelligence with top-tier organizations, and contribute your expertise to shaping the future of the field. As an expert, you play a pivotal role in driving cybersecurity initiatives forward and influencing industry standards. Responsible disclosure programs become a central focus. You'll work closely with software vendors, government agencies, and cybersecurity organizations to coordinate the responsible reporting and patching of advanced vulnerabilities. Your expertise ensures that these programs operate effectively and responsibly. Leadership roles within your organization await you. You become a trusted advisor, guiding your organization's cybersecurity strategy at the highest level. Your ability to communicate complex concepts and risks to executives and stakeholders is essential in shaping security initiatives. In summary, mastering advanced exploitation techniques represents the pinnacle of expertise in the world of cybersecurity. You've explored the evolution of zero-day exploits, advanced exploitation frameworks, privilege escalation, and persistence techniques. You've navigated ethical and legal complexities, proactively defended against emerging threats, engaged in high-level collaboration, and contributed to responsible disclosure efforts. As a master of advanced exploitation, you're not only a defender of digital assets but also a pioneer shaping the future of cybersecurity. Your knowledge and expertise are instrumental in protecting against the most formidable and sophisticated cyber threats, making the digital world a safer place for all.

Chapter 3: Zero Day Discovery and Research Methodologies

In the realm of cybersecurity, the pursuit of knowledge and innovation is a never-ending journey, and as we venture further into the depths of expertise, we arrive at the topic of advanced research methods for zero-day vulnerabilities. By now, you've undoubtedly gained a wealth of experience in identifying, analyzing, and mitigating vulnerabilities. You've explored the intricate world of zero-day exploits, mastered advanced exploitation techniques, and navigated the complex ethical and legal landscape of cybersecurity. Now, it's time to delve into the realm of advanced research, where you'll uncover the most elusive and dangerous vulnerabilities. The first facet of advanced research methods for zero-day vulnerabilities is reconnaissance. This phase involves gathering intelligence about potential targets, including software applications, systems, and networks. You'll learn advanced techniques for open-source intelligence (OSINT) gathering, which allow you to discover valuable information about target organizations and their digital footprint. Additionally, you'll explore the art of passive reconnaissance, which involves collecting data without directly interacting with the target. This approach is crucial for staying covert and avoiding detection by potential adversaries. Advanced vulnerability discovery techniques are at the core of your research journey. You'll delve into the world of fuzz testing, where you subject software applications to a barrage of malformed inputs to uncover hidden vulnerabilities. Your expertise in fuzz testing extends beyond basic techniques; you'll develop custom fuzzers tailored to specific targets, which significantly increase your chances of discovering zero-day vulnerabilities. Furthermore, you'll explore the world of symbolic execution and symbolic reasoning, which allows you to analyze software execution paths systematically. These advanced methods are instrumental in identifying vulnerabilities that elude traditional testing approaches. Another critical aspect of advanced research is reverse engineering. You'll learn how to dissect and analyze software binaries to uncover hidden vulnerabilities. Reverse engineering is essential for understanding how software operates at a low level and how attackers can exploit it. Advanced static code analysis techniques become your secret weapon. You'll use state-of-the-art static analysis tools to scrutinize source code and binaries for vulnerabilities. Your ability to identify intricate code patterns and potential security weaknesses sets you apart as an expert researcher. Advanced dynamic analysis methods allow you to explore the runtime behavior of software applications. You'll use advanced debugging and dynamic analysis tools to monitor software execution, intercept network traffic, and identify vulnerabilities in real-time. These techniques are crucial for uncovering zero-day vulnerabilities that manifest during runtime. Advanced protocol analysis is also an essential part of your research arsenal. You'll delve into the inner workings of network protocols, dissecting packet captures to uncover potential security flaws. Your expertise in this area enables you to identify vulnerabilities that could lead to remote code execution or data breaches. As an advanced researcher, you'll have a deep understanding of binary exploitation. You'll explore advanced techniques such as return-oriented programming (ROP), just-in-time (JIT) exploitation, and advanced heap exploitation. These methods are crucial for crafting reliable and stealthy zero-day exploits. Furthermore, you'll learn about advanced post-exploitation techniques, which allow you to maintain control over compromised systems. Your ability to maintain persistence and evade detection is paramount in advanced research. Ethical considerations remain a guiding principle in your research journey. You'll navigate complex ethical dilemmas as you uncover zero-day vulnerabilities. The responsible disclosure of these vulnerabilities becomes even more critical as your research reaches new heights. You'll collaborate closely with affected organizations and coordinate the responsible disclosure and patching of these vulnerabilities. Your commitment to ethical research practices ensures that your discoveries are used for the greater good and not for malicious purposes. The legal landscape surrounding advanced research methods is intricate, and you'll become well-versed in the legal boundaries and protections afforded to researchers. Understanding the legal aspects of vulnerability research and disclosure is essential for maintaining professional integrity. Collaboration and information sharing take on new dimensions in your advanced research journey. You'll actively engage with top-tier cybersecurity experts, share insights, and contribute to the global defense against cyber threats. Your expertise is highly sought after, and your contributions to research projects and initiatives shape the future of cybersecurity. As you progress in your research, you'll gain recognition as a thought leader and influencer in the field. In summary, advanced research methods for zero-day vulnerabilities represent the pinnacle of your expertise in cybersecurity. You've explored reconnaissance techniques, advanced vulnerability discovery methods, reverse engineering, static and dynamic code analysis, protocol analysis, binary exploitation, and advanced post-exploitation tactics. Ethical considerations, legal awareness, collaboration, and information sharing are central to your research journey. Your expertise is instrumental in uncovering the most elusive and dangerous vulnerabilities, contributing to a safer digital world, and pushing the boundaries of cybersecurity knowledge. Your journey as an advanced researcher is a testament to your dedication to the field and your commitment to protecting digital landscapes from emerging threats.

As you continue your journey into the realm of cybersecurity, you'll encounter a fascinating and ever-evolving field—the exploration of cutting-edge techniques in zero-day discovery. By now, you've accumulated a wealth of knowledge and expertise in various aspects of cybersecurity, from vulnerability identification to advanced research methods. Now, it's time to focus on the forefront of cybersecurity innovation—zero-day discovery. Zero-day vulnerabilities are among the most coveted and dangerous in the digital world, and uncovering them requires a blend of creativity, technical prowess, and a deep understanding of software and systems. Cutting-edge techniques in zero-day discovery empower you to unveil these hidden vulnerabilities and strengthen the digital defenses of organizations and individuals. One of the fundamental aspects of cutting-edge zero-day discovery is the art of target selection. You'll delve into advanced target profiling and selection methods, allowing you to identify high-value targets with the potential for impactful discoveries. Your ability to discern which systems and applications are most likely to harbor zero-day vulnerabilities is a crucial skill in this endeavor. Advanced reconnaissance techniques play a pivotal role in your zero-day discovery journey. You'll explore the world of active reconnaissance, which involves actively probing and scanning target systems for weaknesses. Additionally, you'll master the art of passive reconnaissance, where you collect valuable information about targets without directly engaging with them. This dual approach enhances your stealth and minimizes the risk of detection. Cutting-edge vulnerability discovery techniques are at the heart of your exploration. You'll dive into the world of advanced fuzz testing, where you subject software applications to a relentless barrage of malformed inputs, seeking vulnerabilities that elude traditional testing methods. Your expertise in developing custom fuzzers tailored to specific targets significantly increases your chances of discovering zero-day vulnerabilities. Furthermore, you'll explore the realm of symbolic execution and symbolic reasoning, advanced techniques that enable you to analyze software execution paths systematically. These methods are instrumental in identifying vulnerabilities that hide within complex code structures. Advanced reverse engineering becomes second nature to you. You'll dissect software binaries with precision, unraveling their inner workings to uncover hidden vulnerabilities. Reverse engineering is a crucial skill for understanding how software operates at the lowest levels and how attackers might exploit it. Advanced static code analysis techniques further augment your capabilities. You'll use state-of-the-art static analysis tools to scrutinize source code and binaries, identifying vulnerabilities and security weaknesses that escape conventional inspection. Your ability to discern intricate code patterns and potential vulnerabilities sets you apart as a cutting-edge researcher. Advanced dynamic analysis methods allow you to explore software behavior in real-time. You'll employ advanced debugging and dynamic analysis tools to monitor software execution, intercept network traffic, and identify vulnerabilities as they manifest. These techniques are invaluable for discovering zero-day vulnerabilities that only become apparent during runtime. Advanced protocol analysis takes your skills to the next level. You'll delve into the intricacies of network protocols, dissecting packet captures to identify potential security flaws. Your expertise in this area enables you to uncover vulnerabilities that could lead to remote code execution or data breaches. Cutting-edge post-exploitation techniques are crucial for maintaining control over compromised systems. You'll explore advanced methods for maintaining persistence, evading detection, and exfiltrating sensitive data. Your ability to adapt and innovate in this ever-changing landscape is a testament to your expertise. Ethical considerations continue to be a guiding principle in your work. You'll navigate complex ethical dilemmas as you uncover zero-day vulnerabilities. The responsible disclosure of these vulnerabilities is paramount, and you'll collaborate closely with affected organizations to ensure they are patched promptly and responsibly. Your commitment to ethical research practices ensures that your discoveries are used for the greater good. The legal landscape surrounding cutting-edge zero-day discovery is intricate, and you'll become well-versed in the legal boundaries and protections afforded to researchers. Understanding the legal aspects of vulnerability research and disclosure is essential for maintaining professional integrity. Collaboration and information sharing reach a new level of sophistication. You're actively engaged with top-tier cybersecurity experts, sharing insights, and contributing to global efforts to defend against emerging threats. Your expertise is highly sought after, and your contributions to research projects and initiatives shape the future of cybersecurity. In summary, cutting-edge techniques in zero-day discovery represent the pinnacle of your expertise in the field of cybersecurity. You've honed your skills in target selection, reconnaissance, advanced vulnerability discovery, reverse engineering, static and dynamic code analysis, protocol analysis, binary exploitation, and post-exploitation tactics. Ethical considerations, legal awareness, collaboration, and information sharing are central to your work. Your expertise is instrumental in uncovering the most elusive and dangerous vulnerabilities, contributing to a safer digital world, and pushing the boundaries of cybersecurity knowledge. Your journey as a cutting-edge researcher is a testament to your dedication to the field and your commitment to protecting digital landscapes from emerging threats.

Chapter 4: Advanced Vulnerability Assessment Tools

As you continue your journey into the realm of cybersecurity, you'll encounter the powerful and sophisticated domain of high-level vulnerability assessment solutions. By now, you've acquired a vast range of knowledge and expertise in various aspects of cybersecurity, from foundational concepts to advanced techniques in vulnerability discovery and exploitation. Now, it's time to explore the cutting-edge tools and methodologies that can help organizations identify, prioritize, and mitigate vulnerabilities at a high level. High-level vulnerability assessment solutions are instrumental in the ongoing battle against cyber threats, providing organizations with the means to assess and enhance their security posture comprehensively. One of the key components of high-level vulnerability assessment solutions is their ability to conduct thorough and continuous scanning of an organization's IT infrastructure. These solutions use advanced scanning techniques to identify potential vulnerabilities in network devices, servers, applications, and even cloud-based resources. With high-level vulnerability assessment tools, you can gain a holistic view of your organization's security landscape, pinpointing weaknesses that could be exploited by attackers. These solutions often incorporate automated vulnerability detection algorithms that leverage extensive databases of known vulnerabilities. However, what sets high-level solutions apart is their capability to identify emerging and zero-day vulnerabilities, which might not yet be cataloged in public databases. This level of sophistication enables organizations to stay ahead of cyber threats and respond promptly to newly discovered vulnerabilities. The advanced reporting features of high-level vulnerability assessment solutions are another hallmark of their effectiveness. These solutions generate comprehensive reports that provide detailed insights into identified vulnerabilities. These reports often include information about the severity of each vulnerability, potential impact on the organization, and recommended remediation steps. Moreover, high-level solutions offer prioritization features, helping organizations focus on addressing the most critical vulnerabilities first. This strategic approach is essential in managing resources efficiently and reducing the organization's overall risk exposure. High-level vulnerability assessment solutions often incorporate advanced risk assessment and scoring mechanisms. These mechanisms take into account various factors, such as the asset's importance, the potential impact of an attack, and the likelihood of exploitation. By combining these factors, organizations can assign risk scores to vulnerabilities, allowing them to make informed decisions about which vulnerabilities to address urgently. Moreover, these solutions provide a holistic view of an organization's risk landscape, helping security teams allocate resources effectively. Continuous monitoring and real-time alerting are integral features of high-level vulnerability assessment solutions. These solutions continuously scan the organization's IT environment, ensuring that any newly introduced vulnerabilities are promptly identified. Real-time alerts notify security teams of critical vulnerabilities or unusual activities, enabling rapid response and mitigation. The integration capabilities of high-level vulnerability assessment solutions are vital in today's complex IT environments. These solutions often offer seamless integration with other security tools, such as SIEM (Security Information and Event Management) systems, ticketing systems, and asset management platforms. This integration streamlines the vulnerability management process, making it more efficient and collaborative. Moreover, high-level solutions often support multi-cloud and hybrid environments, ensuring comprehensive coverage in today's diverse IT landscapes. High-level vulnerability assessment solutions are also known for their scalability and adaptability. Organizations of all sizes can leverage these solutions, from small businesses to large enterprises. They can be tailored to suit the specific needs and complexities of the organization's IT infrastructure. This adaptability is essential in ensuring that vulnerability assessment aligns with the organization's unique security requirements. Another standout feature of high-level solutions is their ability to provide actionable insights and recommendations. These solutions not only identify vulnerabilities but also offer guidance on how to remediate them effectively. This guidance may include detailed steps, best practices, and references to security standards and frameworks. Security teams can use these recommendations to streamline the remediation process and enhance their cybersecurity posture. High-level vulnerability assessment solutions are continuously updated to stay ahead of evolving threats. Vulnerability databases are regularly updated with information about newly discovered vulnerabilities and potential exploitation techniques. This proactive approach ensures that organizations are equipped to address the latest security challenges. High-level vulnerability assessment solutions also support compliance initiatives. Many organizations must adhere to industry-specific regulations and standards that mandate regular vulnerability assessments. These solutions facilitate compliance by providing reports and documentation that demonstrate the organization's commitment to security best practices. In summary, leveraging high-level vulnerability assessment solutions represents a significant advancement in an organization's cybersecurity strategy. These solutions offer comprehensive scanning, advanced vulnerability detection, prioritization, risk assessment, continuous monitoring, integration capabilities, scalability, adaptability, actionable insights, and compliance support. By incorporating high-level solutions into their security arsenal, organizations can proactively manage and mitigate vulnerabilities, reduce risk, and fortify their defenses against an ever-evolving threat landscape.

In your ongoing journey through the intricate world of cybersecurity, you've reached a pivotal juncture where you'll explore the art of maximizing the potential of advanced assessment tools. By now, you've undoubtedly developed a robust foundation of knowledge in various cybersecurity domains, from understanding software vulnerabilities to mastering the intricacies of vulnerability assessment. Now, it's time to delve deeper into the realm of advanced assessment tools and harness their capabilities to fortify the digital defenses of organizations and individuals alike. Advanced assessment tools represent a significant leap forward in the realm of cybersecurity, offering a sophisticated array of features and functionalities that can empower security professionals like you. One of the key aspects that distinguish advanced assessment tools is their adaptability and versatility. These tools are designed to accommodate a wide range of environments, from small-scale networks to large, complex infrastructures. They can be tailored to suit the specific needs of the organization, ensuring that the assessment process aligns with its unique IT landscape. Moreover, advanced assessment tools are well-equipped to handle diverse technology stacks, operating systems, and applications, making them indispensable in today's heterogeneous computing environments. The precision and comprehensiveness of these tools are a testament to their advanced nature. They are engineered to provide thorough assessments of an organization's digital assets, leaving no stone unturned. Whether it's scanning network devices, servers, web applications, or cloud-based resources, advanced assessment tools excel in identifying vulnerabilities across the entire IT spectrum. This level of comprehensiveness enables security teams to gain a holistic view of their security posture and make well-informed decisions. Advanced assessment tools are known for their efficiency and speed. They can conduct assessments rapidly, allowing organizations to assess their security posture frequently and respond to emerging threats promptly. This agility is crucial in today's dynamic threat landscape, where vulnerabilities can be exploited in a matter of hours or even minutes. The ability to generate detailed and actionable reports is a hallmark of advanced assessment tools. These tools provide security teams with comprehensive reports that detail identified vulnerabilities, their severity levels, potential impacts, and recommended remediation steps. These reports serve as a roadmap for organizations to prioritize their remediation efforts effectively, focusing on the most critical vulnerabilities first. Additionally, advanced assessment tools often incorporate risk assessment and scoring mechanisms. These mechanisms consider various factors, such as the asset's importance, the likelihood of exploitation, and the potential impact of a successful attack. By assigning risk scores to vulnerabilities, organizations can strategically allocate resources to mitigate the most significant risks, reducing their overall exposure. Automation and integration capabilities are at the forefront of advanced assessment tools. These tools can be seamlessly integrated into an organization's existing cybersecurity infrastructure, such as SIEM (Security Information and Event Management) systems, ticketing platforms, and asset management solutions. Integration streamlines the vulnerability management process, enhancing collaboration among security teams and optimizing resource utilization. The automation of repetitive tasks, such as scanning and reporting, frees up security professionals to focus on more strategic activities, such as vulnerability analysis and threat response. Advanced assessment tools also excel in scalability. They can accommodate the needs of organizations of all sizes, from small businesses to large enterprises. Their scalability ensures that vulnerability assessments remain effective as organizations grow and their IT environments evolve. Furthermore, these tools are continually updated to stay abreast of emerging threats. Their vulnerability databases are regularly updated with information about newly discovered vulnerabilities, potential exploitation techniques, and recommended remediation measures. This proactive approach ensures that organizations are well-equipped to defend against the latest cybersecurity challenges. Advanced assessment tools are indispensable for compliance efforts. Many organizations must adhere to industry-specific regulations and standards that mandate regular vulnerability assessments. These tools generate reports and documentation that serve as evidence of an organization's commitment to cybersecurity best practices, facilitating compliance initiatives. Moreover, advanced assessment tools are designed with the future in mind. They anticipate emerging trends in technology and cybersecurity, ensuring that they remain relevant and effective in the ever-evolving digital landscape. In summary, maximizing the potential of advanced assessment tools represents a significant step forward in the field of cybersecurity. These tools offer adaptability, precision, comprehensiveness, efficiency, detailed reporting, risk assessment, automation, integration, scalability, proactive updates, and compliance support. By harnessing the capabilities of advanced assessment tools, organizations can proactively manage vulnerabilities, reduce risk, and enhance their overall cybersecurity posture in an increasingly complex and dynamic digital world.

Chapter 5: Exploiting Zero Day Vulnerabilities Ethically

As you delve deeper into the realm of advanced exploitation techniques, it's essential to navigate the intricate landscape of ethical considerations that accompany this expertise. Throughout your journey in cybersecurity, you've acquired knowledge and skills that empower you to understand vulnerabilities, discover potential exploits, and develop strategies to safeguard digital ecosystems. Now, as you explore advanced exploitation, you must also understand the ethical implications and responsibilities that come with this knowledge. Ethical considerations in advanced exploitation are paramount, as they determine how your skills are applied and the impact they have on individuals, organizations, and society as a whole. First and foremost, it's vital to emphasize the ethical principles of responsible disclosure. When you uncover a vulnerability or an exploit, your actions should prioritize responsible disclosure, which involves reporting the findings to the affected parties or the appropriate authorities. Responsible disclosure allows organizations to address vulnerabilities and protect their systems before malicious actors can exploit them. It's crucial to refrain from unauthorized or malicious activities, such as hacking, cracking, or exploiting systems without proper authorization. Engaging in such activities is not only unethical but also illegal and can result in severe legal consequences. Ethical hackers, also known as white-hat hackers, adhere to strict ethical guidelines in their actions. They use their skills to identify vulnerabilities, report them responsibly, and assist organizations in improving their security measures. Ethical hackers play a critical role in strengthening the cybersecurity landscape, and their work aligns with the greater good of protecting digital systems from malicious attacks. Moreover, when you come across sensitive or personal data during your vulnerability analysis or exploitation research, it's imperative to handle this information with the utmost care and respect for privacy. Unauthorized access to, sharing, or misuse of personal data is not only unethical but also illegal, as it can violate privacy laws and regulations. Ethical considerations extend to the principle of "do no harm." Your actions in the realm of advanced exploitation should not cause harm to individuals or organizations. Even if you discover vulnerabilities, it's crucial to ensure that your actions do not lead to data breaches, system failures, or any form of harm to the target systems. Ethical hackers prioritize the security and safety of digital ecosystems, and their actions are guided by a commitment to minimizing harm. Another ethical aspect to consider is the distinction between ethical hacking and cybercrime. While ethical hackers operate within the boundaries of the law and ethical guidelines, cybercriminals engage in malicious activities with the intent to steal, damage, or exploit systems and data for personal gain. Understanding this distinction is essential, as it determines the ethical stance of your actions and the consequences they may entail. Furthermore, ethical hackers often operate under explicit agreements and authorizations, such as penetration testing contracts or bug bounty programs. These agreements define the scope, boundaries, and rules of engagement for vulnerability assessment and exploitation. Respecting the terms of these agreements is not only ethical but also a legal requirement. Failure to do so can result in legal repercussions and damage to your professional reputation. In addition to responsible disclosure, ethical hackers should consider the impact of their findings on the affected parties. When reporting vulnerabilities, it's essential to provide clear and detailed information to assist organizations in remediation efforts. Ethical hackers should maintain open and constructive communication with the organizations they assist, offering guidance and support in addressing security weaknesses. Furthermore, ethical hackers should avoid publicizing or sharing sensitive information about vulnerabilities or exploits before they are properly mitigated. Premature disclosure can lead to widespread exploitation by malicious actors and may harm innocent parties. Ethical considerations also extend to the concept of "hacking back" or retaliatory actions against attackers. Engaging in retaliatory activities, even in response to a cyberattack, can have legal and ethical consequences. It's essential to work with law enforcement and legal authorities to address cybercrimes rather than taking matters into your own hands. In summary, ethical considerations are an integral part of advanced exploitation techniques in cybersecurity. As you advance your skills in this field, it's crucial to uphold ethical principles, such as responsible disclosure, respecting privacy, avoiding unauthorized access, and prioritizing the greater good of securing digital ecosystems. Ethical hackers play a vital role in safeguarding the digital world, and their actions should align with the highest ethical standards to promote a safer and more secure online environment for all.

Navigating the delicate balance between security research and responsible disclosure is a fundamental aspect of the ethical framework that guides cybersecurity professionals. As you've ventured deeper into the world of cybersecurity, you've likely encountered scenarios where your knowledge and skills can uncover vulnerabilities and weaknesses in digital systems. While this expertise empowers you to enhance security, it also comes with a set of ethical considerations and responsibilities. Security research involves the exploration of digital environments to identify vulnerabilities, weaknesses, and potential threats. It's a critical aspect of cybersecurity that enables professionals to understand and address vulnerabilities before they can be exploited by malicious actors. Responsible disclosure, on the other hand, is the ethical practice of reporting these vulnerabilities to the relevant parties, such as the organization responsible for the affected system. The balance between security research and responsible disclosure is crucial, as it determines how your actions impact the security of digital ecosystems and the organizations or individuals relying on them. One key principle of responsible disclosure is transparency. When you discover a vulnerability, it's essential to be transparent about your findings, your intentions, and your willingness to collaborate with the affected parties to mitigate the issue. Open and honest communication fosters trust and cooperation, allowing organizations to take prompt action to secure their systems. The responsible disclosure process often involves coordination with the organization's security team, IT personnel, or designated contact. This collaboration ensures that the vulnerability is accurately understood, verified, and addressed in a timely manner. Security researchers should also provide detailed information about the vulnerability, including its severity, potential impacts, and steps to reproduce it. This level of detail assists organizations in assessing the risk and prioritizing their remediation efforts effectively. In some cases, security researchers may choose to follow established vulnerability disclosure programs, such as bug bounty programs. These programs provide clear guidelines and procedures for reporting vulnerabilities, and they often offer rewards or compensation to researchers who discover and responsibly disclose security issues. Bug bounty programs create a structured and mutually beneficial environment for security researchers and organizations. While responsible disclosure is a cornerstone of ethical security research, there are situations where it becomes more complex. Some organizations may be unresponsive or slow to address reported vulnerabilities, potentially leaving their systems exposed to exploitation. In such cases, security researchers may face ethical dilemmas regarding when and how to disclose the vulnerability to the public or the broader cybersecurity community. The decision to engage in full disclosure, which involves publicly revealing the vulnerability, should be made carefully and as a last resort. Full disclosure can have significant consequences, as it may lead to immediate exploitation by malicious actors if the affected party does not take action. Security researchers should consider the potential harm and consequences of full disclosure, weighing them against the urgency of addressing the vulnerability. Additionally, it's important to be aware of legal considerations when conducting security research and responsible disclosure. Laws and regulations related to cybersecurity can vary by jurisdiction, and security researchers should ensure that their actions comply with relevant legal requirements. Engaging in unauthorized access, data breaches, or other illegal activities can lead to legal consequences, even if the intentions are ethical. Moreover, responsible disclosure extends to the protection of personal data and privacy. Security researchers should handle any sensitive or personal information they encounter during their research with the utmost care, adhering to privacy laws and ethical guidelines. Respecting the privacy of individuals is a fundamental aspect of responsible cybersecurity research. Ethical security researchers also recognize the importance of continuous education and professional development. They stay informed about the latest trends in cybersecurity, emerging threats, and evolving best practices. This commitment to learning ensures that their research and disclosure practices remain effective and aligned with industry standards. In summary, balancing security research and responsible disclosure is a vital aspect of the ethical framework that guides cybersecurity professionals. It involves transparency, collaboration with organizations, adherence to established vulnerability disclosure programs, and careful consideration of the consequences of full disclosure. Responsible security research contributes to a safer digital environment, and ethical researchers play a crucial role in protecting digital ecosystems and the individuals and organizations that rely on them.

Chapter 6: Advanced Reporting and Documentation

As you progress in your journey of vulnerability analysis, one essential skill you must master is the art of crafting comprehensive reports for advanced vulnerabilities. These reports serve as a bridge of communication between you, as the security expert, and the stakeholders responsible for mitigating the identified vulnerabilities. A well-crafted report not only conveys the technical details of the vulnerability but also provides the necessary context and guidance for remediation. The process of creating comprehensive reports begins with understanding the audience. Consider who will be reading the report, their technical expertise, and their specific roles in the remediation process. Tailoring your report to the audience's level of understanding is crucial for effective communication. For technical audiences, you can delve into the technical details of the vulnerability, including the specific code or configuration issues that were identified. However, for non-technical stakeholders, it's essential to present the information in a clear and accessible manner. Begin your report with an executive summary that provides a high-level overview of the vulnerability. This summary should include the severity of the vulnerability, potential impacts, and a concise explanation of the remediation steps required. The executive summary is often the first section that stakeholders read, so it should grab their attention and provide a quick understanding of the situation. After the executive summary, provide detailed technical information about the vulnerability.

This section should include a description of the vulnerability's nature, the affected systems or applications, and the steps to reproduce it. Include any relevant code snippets, logs, or configuration settings that can help the technical team understand the issue. Additionally, provide an assessment of the vulnerability's severity and potential impact. Use a standardized rating system, such as the Common Vulnerability Scoring System (CVSS), to quantify the severity objectively. Explaining the potential impact involves discussing the consequences of the vulnerability being exploited, such as data breaches, system downtime, or unauthorized access. To enhance the comprehensiveness of your report, consider including recommendations for remediation. Provide clear and actionable steps that the organization or technical team can follow to mitigate the vulnerability. These recommendations should address the root cause of the issue and not just provide temporary fixes. Include guidance on configuring security settings, updating software or patches, or making code changes. To further assist the remediation process, offer references to relevant resources, such as official documentation, security advisories, or best practices. Including these references demonstrates your commitment to providing accurate and up-to-date information. In addition to the technical details, consider adding a section on potential attack scenarios. Illustrate how the vulnerability could be exploited by malicious actors to compromise the system or data. This helps stakeholders understand the real-world implications of the vulnerability and motivates them to prioritize remediation. Furthermore, share any insights you may have about the vulnerability's prevalence in the wild. Research whether similar vulnerabilities have been exploited in the past and if there are known instances of attacks targeting this type of vulnerability. Such contextual information can help organizations assess the urgency of remediation. When it comes to crafting comprehensive reports, visuals can be a valuable tool. Consider using diagrams, flowcharts, or graphs to illustrate key points or attack scenarios. Visual aids can make complex concepts more accessible and enhance the overall clarity of the report. While presenting technical details is crucial, don't underestimate the importance of language and tone in your report. Maintain a professional and respectful tone throughout the document. Avoid jargon or overly technical language that might alienate non-technical stakeholders. Use plain language to explain complex concepts, ensuring that even individuals with limited technical knowledge can grasp the essentials. Keep the report organized and structured, using headings and subheadings to divide sections logically. A well-structured report is easier to navigate and ensures that readers can quickly find the information they need. Proofread and edit your report meticulously to eliminate grammatical errors, typos, and inconsistencies. A polished report reflects positively on your professionalism and attention to detail. Before finalizing your report, consider seeking peer review or feedback from colleagues or mentors. Another set of eyes can provide valuable insights and help identify any gaps or areas that need improvement. Lastly, always be prepared to provide additional context or clarification when stakeholders have questions or seek further information. Your role as a vulnerability analyst extends beyond creating reports; you are also a communicator and educator. In summary, crafting comprehensive reports for advanced vulnerabilities is a critical skill in the field of cybersecurity. These reports serve as a vital communication tool that bridges the gap between technical experts and stakeholders responsible for security remediation. By tailoring your reports to the audience, providing technical details, offering remediation recommendations, and maintaining a professional tone, you can effectively convey the importance of mitigating vulnerabilities and contribute to a more secure digital landscape.

As you advance in your journey of vulnerability analysis, documenting advanced vulnerability findings becomes increasingly crucial. Effective documentation is the key to ensuring that your discoveries are communicated clearly, accurately, and comprehensively to the relevant stakeholders. Next, we will delve into the art of documenting advanced vulnerabilities effectively, providing you with the knowledge and techniques needed to excel in this critical aspect of your work. At the heart of documenting advanced vulnerabilities is the goal of providing actionable information to those responsible for mitigating the identified risks. This information should not only describe the vulnerability but also offer guidance on remediation and risk mitigation. The documentation process typically starts with thoroughly understanding the vulnerability you've discovered. This involves delving deep into the technical details, exploring the underlying causes, and assessing the potential impact on the affected systems or applications. Before putting pen to paper (or fingers to keyboard), it's essential to gather all the necessary information. This includes not only the technical specifics of the vulnerability but also contextual information, such as the affected software versions, configuration settings, and any associated threat vectors. A structured approach to documenting vulnerabilities is essential to ensure consistency and completeness in your reports. Consider creating a template or checklist that you can follow for each vulnerability assessment. Such a template can include sections for the vulnerability's title, identifier (if available), description, technical details, potential impact, risk assessment, and remediation steps. The title should be concise and descriptive, providing a clear indication of the nature of the vulnerability. The identifier, if applicable, is a unique reference that can be useful for tracking and cross-referencing vulnerabilities. In the description section, provide a high-level overview of the vulnerability. Explain what the vulnerability is, how it can be exploited, and what potential consequences could arise from exploitation. The technical details section is where you dive deep into the specifics of the vulnerability. This may include code snippets, proof-of-concept examples, or detailed explanations of the vulnerability's inner workings. Remember to document any known variations or nuances of the vulnerability to provide a comprehensive view. When assessing potential impact, consider the severity of the vulnerability and its implications for the affected systems. Use a standardized rating system, such as the Common Vulnerability Scoring System (CVSS), to quantify the severity objectively. Discuss the potential consequences, such as data breaches, system compromise, or service disruptions. Risk assessment is an essential component of vulnerability documentation. Evaluate the likelihood of exploitation and the potential impact on business operations or data security. This assessment helps stakeholders prioritize remediation efforts. Effective documentation includes clear and actionable remediation steps. Provide specific guidance on how to mitigate the vulnerability, including configuration changes, software updates, or code fixes. In some cases, it may be necessary to offer alternative solutions or workarounds while a permanent fix is being implemented. Whenever possible, reference official documentation, security advisories, or best practices to support your recommendations. Adding references lends credibility to your documentation and ensures that stakeholders have access to the most up-to-date information. While the technical aspects are crucial, don't neglect the human element in your documentation. Consider including a section on attack scenarios, where you outline how an attacker could exploit the vulnerability in real-world situations. This helps stakeholders understand the practical implications of the vulnerability and motivates them to take action. In addition to documenting the vulnerability itself, be sure to include any additional context or insights you've gathered during your analysis. This might include information about similar vulnerabilities, known exploits in the wild, or any patterns you've observed in your research. Such context can assist stakeholders in making informed decisions regarding remediation priorities. Visual aids, such as diagrams or flowcharts, can enhance your documentation by illustrating key points or attack scenarios. Use these aids sparingly and only when they add value to the understanding of the vulnerability. Maintain a professional and respectful tone throughout your documentation. Avoid jargon or overly technical language that might alienate non-technical stakeholders. Use plain language to explain complex concepts, ensuring that even individuals with limited technical knowledge can grasp the essentials. Organize your documentation logically, using headings and subheadings to structure the content. A well-organized document is easier to navigate and ensures that readers can quickly find the information they need. Proofread and edit your documentation carefully to eliminate grammatical errors, typos, or inconsistencies. A polished document reflects positively on your professionalism and attention to detail. Consider seeking peer review or feedback from colleagues or mentors before finalizing your documentation. Another perspective can provide valuable insights and help identify any gaps or areas that need improvement. Lastly, always be prepared to provide additional context or clarification when stakeholders have questions or seek further information. Your role as a vulnerability analyst extends beyond just creating reports; you are also a communicator and educator. In summary, documenting advanced vulnerability findings effectively is a critical skill in the field of cybersecurity. It ensures that your discoveries are communicated clearly and comprehensively to the relevant stakeholders, ultimately contributing to a more secure digital landscape.

Chapter 7: Cutting-Edge Remediation Strategies

As we delve deeper into the realm of vulnerability analysis, it becomes increasingly evident that traditional remediation approaches may not always suffice. In this chapter, we will explore the concept of implementing innovative remediation approaches, which are designed to address vulnerabilities in a more dynamic and proactive manner. While conventional remediation methods focus on patching or updating vulnerable software, innovative approaches consider a broader spectrum of solutions. These solutions not only aim to fix the immediate issue but also work towards preventing similar vulnerabilities from emerging in the future. One such innovative approach is the concept of self-healing systems. These systems are designed to automatically detect and remediate vulnerabilities without human intervention. They use advanced algorithms and machine learning to identify anomalies or suspicious activities in real-time and take immediate action to mitigate the threat. Self-healing systems are particularly valuable in environments where rapid response to vulnerabilities is critical, such as in critical infrastructure or healthcare systems. Another innovative remediation approach involves the use of containerization and microservices architecture. This approach isolates individual components of an application into separate containers, making it easier to patch or update specific parts without affecting the entire system. Containers allow for rapid deployment of updates and can reduce downtime during the remediation process. Moreover, microservices architecture promotes modularization, making it easier to identify and remediate vulnerabilities in isolated components. Moving away from a reactive stance, innovative remediation approaches also emphasize proactive security measures. One such measure is the concept of "shift left" in software development. Traditionally, security assessments and vulnerability remediation were performed late in the software development lifecycle. However, the shift-left approach integrates security from the very beginning of the development process. Developers are trained to write secure code, and automated security testing tools are used throughout the development pipeline. This proactive approach significantly reduces the likelihood of vulnerabilities appearing in the final product, saving time and resources on remediation efforts later. Additionally, vulnerability management and remediation platforms are evolving to incorporate more innovative features. These platforms leverage artificial intelligence and machine learning to prioritize vulnerabilities based on risk and potential impact. By analyzing data from various sources, such as threat intelligence feeds and historical vulnerability data, these platforms can help organizations focus their remediation efforts on the most critical issues. Another innovative remediation approach is threat modeling, which involves identifying potential threats and vulnerabilities in the early stages of application or system design. By analyzing the system's architecture and potential attack vectors, security experts can proactively address vulnerabilities before they are even introduced. Threat modeling provides valuable insights into the security posture of a system and guides the implementation of appropriate security controls. One of the key challenges in implementing innovative remediation approaches is the need for skilled professionals who can design, implement, and manage these solutions effectively. This highlights the importance of investing in cybersecurity talent development and training programs. Organizations should prioritize the acquisition of talent capable of understanding and harnessing innovative remediation technologies. Additionally, regulatory compliance requirements may play a significant role in driving the adoption of innovative remediation approaches. Many regulations and industry standards now emphasize the importance of proactive security measures and rapid vulnerability remediation. Organizations that fail to keep pace with these evolving requirements may face legal and reputational consequences. Ultimately, the adoption of innovative remediation approaches requires a shift in mindset from reactive to proactive security. It involves recognizing that vulnerabilities are not isolated incidents but symptoms of larger systemic issues. By addressing the root causes and implementing proactive security measures, organizations can reduce their exposure to vulnerabilities and improve their overall security posture. In summary, implementing innovative remediation approaches is essential in today's dynamic and evolving cybersecurity landscape. These approaches offer a proactive and holistic way to address vulnerabilities and enhance overall security. While they may require initial investments in technology and talent development, the long-term benefits in terms of reduced risk and improved resilience make them a worthwhile endeavor for organizations seeking to stay ahead of emerging threats.

In our journey through the intricate landscape of vulnerability analysis and resolution, we have explored various aspects of identifying, prioritizing, and mitigating vulnerabilities. However, as we ascend to more advanced levels of expertise, it becomes crucial to delve into advanced techniques for vulnerability resolution. These techniques are designed to address vulnerabilities in a more sophisticated and strategic manner, considering not only immediate fixes but also long-term security improvements. One of the advanced techniques in vulnerability resolution is the concept of "virtual patching." Virtual patching involves the implementation of security measures at the network or application layer to mitigate the risk posed by a vulnerability without modifying the vulnerable software itself. This technique can be especially valuable when immediate patching is not feasible due to various constraints, such as compatibility issues, time-sensitive operations, or the unavailability of a vendor-supplied patch. Virtual patching can be achieved through the deployment of Intrusion Prevention Systems (IPS) or Web Application Firewalls (WAFs) that are configured to detect and block attempted exploits targeting known vulnerabilities. These security controls act as a shield, intercepting malicious traffic and preventing it from reaching the vulnerable application. Another advanced technique in vulnerability resolution involves the use of "compensating controls." Compensating controls are security measures or safeguards put in place to substitute for the unavailability or impracticality of implementing the primary security control. In the context of vulnerability resolution, compensating controls can be employed when applying a patch or update is not immediately possible, and the risk must be mitigated through alternative means. For example, if a critical vulnerability is discovered in an essential system, but applying a patch would disrupt critical operations, organizations may implement additional network segmentation, access controls, or monitoring to mitigate the risk until a suitable patch can be applied safely. These compensating controls are temporary solutions that help bridge the security gap until a more permanent resolution can be implemented. Advanced techniques in vulnerability resolution also encompass the concept of "security by design." This approach entails integrating security considerations into the entire software development lifecycle, from design and development to testing and deployment. Security by design requires organizations to adopt secure coding practices, conduct thorough security reviews, and incorporate security testing into the development process. By embedding security into the software development process, vulnerabilities can be proactively prevented, significantly reducing the need for post-release patches and updates. Additionally, organizations can employ "vulnerability orchestration" as an advanced technique in vulnerability resolution. Vulnerability orchestration platforms automate and streamline the vulnerability management process, from identification to resolution. These platforms integrate with various security tools and systems, aggregating vulnerability data, prioritizing risks, and orchestrating remediation actions. By automating routine tasks and decision-making processes, vulnerability orchestration helps security teams respond to vulnerabilities more efficiently and consistently. Furthermore, organizations can explore the concept of "red teaming" as an advanced technique in vulnerability resolution. Red teaming involves simulating real-world cyberattacks on an organization's systems, applications, and networks to identify vulnerabilities and weaknesses. Red teams, comprised of skilled cybersecurity professionals, attempt to exploit vulnerabilities in a controlled and ethical manner, providing valuable insights into an organization's security posture. The findings from red team exercises can guide organizations in prioritizing and addressing vulnerabilities effectively. To achieve advanced vulnerability resolution, organizations may also consider the adoption of "DevSecOps" practices. DevSecOps integrates security into the DevOps (Development and Operations) process, ensuring that security is a fundamental aspect of the continuous integration and continuous deployment (CI/CD) pipeline. By automating security testing and validation throughout the development process, organizations can identify and resolve vulnerabilities at an earlier stage, reducing the need for post-release patches. Advanced techniques in vulnerability resolution require organizations to adopt a proactive and strategic approach to security. This involves aligning security practices with business objectives, understanding the unique risks facing the organization, and continuously improving security processes. It also requires investing in the development of security expertise and leveraging advanced tools and technologies. Moreover, organizations should stay informed about emerging threats and vulnerabilities and adapt their vulnerability resolution strategies accordingly. As we navigate the complex terrain of advanced vulnerability resolution, it becomes clear that the approach to addressing vulnerabilities should not be one-size-fits-all. Instead, organizations should tailor their strategies to their specific needs, taking into account factors such as risk tolerance, operational requirements, and resource constraints. By embracing advanced techniques and practices, organizations can enhance their ability to identify, prioritize, and mitigate vulnerabilities effectively, ultimately strengthening their overall security posture.

Chapter 8: Advanced Security Practices for Analysts

As we delve deeper into the realm of cybersecurity and vulnerability analysis, it becomes increasingly evident that achieving expert-level proficiency requires a comprehensive understanding of advanced security protocols and practices. Expertise in this domain goes beyond basic vulnerability scanning and patching; it involves mastering a range of security measures and strategies designed to protect an organization's digital assets from sophisticated threats. One fundamental aspect of expert-level security is the adoption of a "defense-in-depth" strategy. Defense-in-depth is a multi-layered security approach that aims to provide multiple layers of protection, making it more challenging for attackers to breach an organization's defenses. These layers can include firewalls, intrusion detection systems, intrusion prevention systems, antivirus software, and robust access controls. By implementing a defense-in-depth strategy, organizations create a formidable barrier against both known and unknown threats. Expert-level security also involves the deployment of advanced authentication methods, such as multi-factor authentication (MFA) and biometric authentication. MFA requires users to provide two or more authentication factors, such as something they know (a password), something they have (a token or smart card), or something they are (biometric data). Biometric authentication, which relies on unique physical or behavioral characteristics like fingerprints or facial recognition, offers a high level of security and is increasingly prevalent in modern systems. Another crucial aspect of expert-level security protocols is the rigorous enforcement of access controls. Access controls determine who can access specific resources or data within an organization's network. Expert security professionals carefully define access permissions, implement role-based access controls (RBAC), and regularly review and update access rights to minimize the risk of unauthorized access. Encryption is another cornerstone of advanced security practices. Data encryption ensures that sensitive information remains confidential and secure, even if it falls into the wrong hands. Expert-level security protocols leverage strong encryption algorithms and ensure that data is encrypted both in transit and at rest. Furthermore, expert security professionals closely monitor network traffic and behavior to detect anomalies and potential security threats. Intrusion detection systems (IDS) and intrusion prevention systems (IPS) play a critical role in this regard. IDSs monitor network traffic for suspicious activity, while IPSs can actively block or mitigate threats when detected. These systems are continuously updated to stay ahead of emerging threats and vulnerabilities. Advanced security practices also involve the development and implementation of a robust incident response plan. An incident response plan outlines the steps to be taken when a security incident or breach occurs. Expert-level organizations not only have a well-defined plan but also conduct regular tabletop exercises and simulations to ensure that their response teams are prepared for various scenarios. Moreover, they establish communication protocols to coordinate with internal and external stakeholders during an incident. Security awareness and training are ongoing initiatives at the expert level. Organizations conduct regular training sessions for employees to educate them about security best practices, common threats, and how to recognize phishing attempts or social engineering attacks. Employees are considered a crucial line of defense, and their vigilance is highly valued. When it comes to protecting against advanced threats, expert-level security practices extend to threat intelligence and threat hunting. Threat intelligence involves gathering and analyzing data about emerging threats, attack techniques, and threat actors. This information is used to proactively strengthen defenses and identify potential vulnerabilities. Threat hunting, on the other hand, is a proactive approach to identifying and mitigating threats that may have evaded traditional security measures. Expert security professionals actively search for signs of malicious activity within their networks and take decisive action to neutralize threats. Expert-level security also encompasses the concept of "zero trust" security. In a zero trust model, no one is trusted by default, whether they are inside or outside the network perimeter. Every user and device must authenticate and continuously verify their trustworthiness before accessing resources. This model is particularly effective in mitigating the risks associated with insider threats and lateral movement by attackers. Furthermore, expert-level security practices align with compliance and regulatory requirements specific to the organization's industry and geographic location. Compliance ensures that security measures are not only effective but also meet legal and industry standards. Expert security professionals work closely with legal and compliance teams to navigate the complex landscape of regulations, such as GDPR, HIPAA, or PCI DSS. Finally, expert-level security is characterized by continuous improvement and adaptation. Security professionals stay up-to-date with the latest threats, vulnerabilities, and technologies. They actively participate in information sharing and collaboration with other security experts and organizations. Moreover, they regularly conduct penetration testing and vulnerability assessments to assess the effectiveness of their security measures. In summary, achieving expert-level proficiency in security protocols and practices is an ongoing journey that demands dedication, vigilance, and a deep understanding of the ever-evolving threat landscape. It requires a multifaceted approach that combines advanced technologies, well-defined processes, and a security-conscious organizational culture. By embracing the principles and practices of expert-level security, organizations can fortify their defenses and effectively safeguard their digital assets in an increasingly complex and interconnected world.

As you advance in your journey as a security analyst, it becomes increasingly vital to focus on enhancing the overall security posture of your organization. Your role evolves beyond merely identifying vulnerabilities and threats; you are now a key player in fortifying the organization's defenses and ensuring its resilience against a constantly evolving threat landscape. One of the first steps in enhancing the security posture is to adopt a proactive mindset. Rather than solely reacting to incidents and vulnerabilities, you actively seek out potential weaknesses in the organization's infrastructure, applications, and processes. This proactive approach involves thorough risk assessments and penetration testing to identify vulnerabilities before they can be exploited by malicious actors. It also includes evaluating the security of third-party vendors and partners who may have access to your organization's data and systems. Collaboration becomes paramount at this stage of your journey. You work closely with cross-functional teams, including IT, development, compliance, and legal departments. Together, you define and implement comprehensive security policies and procedures that align with industry best practices and regulatory requirements. This collaboration extends to incident response planning, where you ensure that every team knows its role and responsibilities in the event of a security breach. Furthermore, you play a crucial role in developing and maintaining security awareness programs for employees. This involves educating staff about the latest threats and attack vectors, as well as promoting a culture of security within the organization. Another essential aspect of enhancing security posture is the implementation of robust access controls. You employ techniques such as role-based access control (RBAC), which assigns permissions based on job roles, and least privilege access, which restricts users' access rights to the minimum necessary for their tasks. This minimizes the attack surface and limits the potential impact of a breach. Advanced analysts also delve into the world of threat intelligence. You keep a close watch on emerging threats, zero-day vulnerabilities, and the tactics, techniques, and procedures (TTPs) of threat actors. By staying informed about the latest developments in the threat landscape, you can proactively adjust security measures to mitigate potential risks. Intrusion detection and prevention systems (IDS/IPS) are essential tools in your arsenal. These systems continuously monitor network traffic and behavior, alerting you to suspicious activities and enabling you to take immediate action to block or contain threats. You fine-tune these systems to reduce false positives and enhance their effectiveness. In addition to safeguarding the network perimeter, you focus on endpoint security. Endpoint detection and response (EDR) solutions become integral in identifying and containing threats on individual devices. Advanced analysts implement and manage EDR solutions to detect malicious activity at the endpoint and respond swiftly to mitigate risks. A critical component of your role is to lead incident response efforts. You coordinate the response to security incidents, ensuring that the organization follows a well-defined incident response plan. This plan includes steps for containment, eradication, recovery, and lessons learned to prevent future incidents. You also establish communication protocols to keep stakeholders informed during an incident, from employees and customers to regulatory authorities and the media. Thorough documentation is key in the world of advanced security analysis. You maintain detailed records of security incidents, vulnerabilities, and remediation efforts. This documentation serves not only for compliance and regulatory purposes but also as a valuable resource for post-incident analysis and continuous improvement. As an advanced analyst, you actively engage in threat hunting. This proactive approach involves actively searching for signs of malicious activity within the organization's network. You use your deep knowledge of the organization's infrastructure and threat intelligence to identify and neutralize threats that may have gone undetected by automated systems. Advanced analysts often embrace the concept of zero trust security. In a zero trust model, trust is never assumed, and verification is required from anyone trying to access resources in the organization's network. This approach helps prevent lateral movement by attackers and strengthens overall security. Finally, you take a leadership role in evaluating and implementing new security technologies and strategies. You stay informed about emerging security trends and assess their potential benefits and risks to the organization. You evaluate new security tools and determine how they can enhance the security posture, whether through artificial intelligence (AI)-driven threat detection, machine learning algorithms, or advanced authentication methods. In summary, advancing your role as an advanced security analyst is a journey that requires a combination of technical expertise, collaboration, and proactive thinking. You play a critical role in not only identifying vulnerabilities and threats but also in fortifying your organization's defenses and ensuring its ability to withstand the ever-evolving challenges of the cybersecurity landscape. By continually enhancing the security posture and staying at the forefront of security best practices, you contribute significantly to the overall resilience and success of your organization.

Chapter 9: Collaborative Approaches to Complex Vulnerabilities

In the world of cybersecurity, collaboration is often the key to successfully tackling complex vulnerabilities. As we delve into this topic, it's essential to understand that no organization is an island. Every entity, regardless of its size or industry, is part of a larger ecosystem that includes partners, suppliers, customers, and even competitors. This interconnectedness means that vulnerabilities in one organization's systems can potentially impact others. Hence, it's crucial to adopt a collaborative approach to address vulnerabilities comprehensively. One of the first steps in collaborative vulnerability management is establishing clear communication channels. Effective communication is the foundation of any successful collaborative effort. Organizations need to create channels through which they can share information about vulnerabilities, threats, and best practices. This communication can take various forms, including email alerts, web portals, and even direct conversations. However, it's essential to establish protocols for sharing sensitive information securely, especially when dealing with critical vulnerabilities. Collaboration also extends to sharing threat intelligence. Many organizations invest in threat intelligence services to gather information about emerging threats and attack trends. By sharing this intelligence within a collaborative network, organizations can collectively stay informed about potential risks. Moreover, organizations can pool their resources to analyze this data more effectively and develop strategies for mitigating shared threats. Collaboration also involves joint vulnerability assessments. Organizations can work together to conduct assessments on common software, platforms, or technologies. These assessments can uncover vulnerabilities that may not be apparent when examined in isolation. The results can then be shared with all parties involved, ensuring that everyone benefits from the collective effort. Another aspect of collaborative vulnerability management is information sharing and analysis centers (ISACs). ISACs are industry-specific organizations that facilitate the sharing of cybersecurity information and best practices among member organizations. Joining an ISAC relevant to your industry can provide valuable insights and early warnings about vulnerabilities and threats specific to your sector. Collaboration can also extend to penetration testing. Some organizations partner with trusted security firms to conduct joint penetration tests. This collaborative approach can simulate real-world attacks and uncover vulnerabilities that internal teams may overlook. Moreover, it allows organizations to share the cost and resources required for comprehensive testing. Collaboration doesn't stop at the organizational level; it also extends to the broader cybersecurity community. Participating in public-private partnerships, information sharing and analysis organizations (ISAOs), and industry-specific forums can provide access to a wealth of knowledge and resources. These collaborative efforts help organizations stay ahead of emerging threats and vulnerabilities. In addition to sharing information and assessments, organizations can collaborate on remediation strategies. When vulnerabilities are discovered, organizations can work together to develop and share mitigation strategies. This includes sharing information about patching schedules, workarounds, and other strategies for reducing the risk posed by vulnerabilities. Collaboration also plays a crucial role in incident response. When a security incident occurs, organizations often need to work together to contain and mitigate the threat. This may involve sharing threat indicators, coordinating responses, and pooling resources to investigate and remediate the incident. Moreover, organizations can benefit from post-incident collaboration by sharing lessons learned and best practices to improve their overall security posture. In the world of collaborative vulnerability management, trust is paramount. Organizations must have confidence in the security and confidentiality of the information they share. Establishing trust can take time, but it's essential for building effective collaborative relationships. One way to build trust is through the use of formal agreements, such as information sharing and non-disclosure agreements (NDAs). These agreements outline the terms and conditions of information sharing, including how sensitive data will be protected and used. Collaboration also requires a commitment to reciprocity. Organizations that benefit from shared information and resources should be willing to reciprocate by sharing their findings and insights. This reciprocity fosters a culture of collaboration and ensures that all parties involved receive value from the partnership. In summary, collaborative strategies for tackling complex vulnerabilities are essential in today's interconnected world. No organization can defend against all threats and vulnerabilities alone. By working together, sharing information, and pooling resources, organizations can strengthen their collective cybersecurity posture. Collaboration not only enhances security but also allows organizations to respond more effectively to emerging threats and vulnerabilities. As you continue your journey in cybersecurity, remember the power of collaboration and the importance of building trust within your network of partners and peers.

In the realm of cybersecurity, orchestrating cross-team collaboration is a critical component of advanced vulnerability mitigation efforts. As organizations face increasingly sophisticated threats and vulnerabilities, a unified approach becomes paramount. Cybersecurity is not the sole responsibility of the IT department; it requires a coordinated effort across various teams and departments within an organization. This chapter will delve into the importance of orchestrating cross-team collaboration, the key players involved, and strategies for effective collaboration. First and foremost, it's essential to recognize that cybersecurity is not a siloed function. Traditionally, IT and cybersecurity teams bore the primary responsibility for safeguarding an organization's digital assets. However, the landscape has evolved, and cybersecurity has become an enterprise-wide concern. The collaborative effort involves multiple teams, including IT, security, development, operations, compliance, legal, and executive leadership. Each of these teams plays a unique role in ensuring that vulnerabilities are identified, assessed, and mitigated effectively. IT teams are on the front lines of cybersecurity, managing the organization's infrastructure and systems. They are responsible for implementing security measures, patching vulnerabilities, and ensuring the day-to-day security of IT assets. Security teams, on the other hand, are focused on threat detection and response. They use tools and techniques to monitor network traffic, identify suspicious activities, and investigate potential security incidents. Development teams are responsible for creating and maintaining software applications. They play a vital role in identifying and addressing vulnerabilities in the software development life cycle (SDLC). Operations teams oversee the deployment and maintenance of applications and services. Their collaboration is crucial in ensuring that security measures are implemented correctly in the production environment. Compliance teams ensure that the organization adheres to relevant regulations and industry standards. Their role is to ensure that security measures are in line with compliance requirements and to report on the organization's adherence to these standards. Legal teams may become involved when incidents or vulnerabilities have legal implications. They help navigate legal aspects, such as breach notification requirements and liability issues. Executive leadership, including the C-suite and the board of directors, sets the strategic direction for cybersecurity. Their buy-in and support are essential for allocating resources and prioritizing cybersecurity efforts. Effective cross-team collaboration begins with clear communication and a shared understanding of goals and objectives. All teams must be aligned in their understanding of the organization's risk tolerance and security priorities. A common language for discussing vulnerabilities and risks should be established, ensuring that technical and non-technical team members can communicate effectively. In many organizations, a formalized governance structure is put in place to facilitate collaboration. This structure typically includes a cross-functional cybersecurity committee or council that meets regularly to discuss security matters. The committee may include representatives from each relevant team and is responsible for making decisions and setting priorities. It's also essential to establish accountability and ownership for vulnerability management. Each team should have a clear understanding of its responsibilities in the vulnerability management process. For example, IT teams may be responsible for patching vulnerabilities, while security teams focus on monitoring and incident response. Development teams should integrate security into the SDLC and conduct code reviews to identify and address vulnerabilities early in the development process. Operations teams play a crucial role in deploying security updates and ensuring that configurations are secure. Collaboration tools and platforms can facilitate communication and information sharing among teams. These tools can include incident tracking systems, project management software, and secure messaging platforms. By providing a centralized place for teams to collaborate, these tools can streamline the vulnerability management process. Automation also plays a significant role in cross-team collaboration. Automated vulnerability scanning and assessment tools can identify vulnerabilities and prioritize them based on risk. These tools can provide actionable information to IT, development, and security teams, allowing them to work together to address the most critical vulnerabilities first. Regular training and awareness programs can help teams stay informed about the latest threats and vulnerabilities. Security awareness training should be provided to all employees, helping them recognize and report security incidents. Technical teams should receive training on secure coding practices and vulnerability assessment techniques. Collaboration doesn't stop at the organizational level; it extends to external partners and vendors. Many organizations rely on third-party vendors for various services, and these vendors may have access to the organization's systems and data. Collaboration with vendors should include assessing their security practices and ensuring that they meet the organization's security standards. Additionally, organizations should have plans in place for responding to incidents involving third-party vendors. In summary, orchestrating cross-team collaboration is a fundamental aspect of advanced vulnerability mitigation. The modern threat landscape requires organizations to work together to identify, assess, and remediate vulnerabilities effectively. Teams across IT, security, development, operations, compliance, legal, and executive leadership must collaborate and communicate to protect the organization's digital assets. Establishing clear accountability, a common language, and a formal governance structure can facilitate this collaboration. Automation, collaboration tools, and training programs can further enhance the effectiveness of cross-team efforts. By working together, organizations can strengthen their cybersecurity posture and better defend against evolving threats and vulnerabilities.

Chapter 10: Mastering Advanced Vulnerability Analysis Techniques

Mastery in advanced vulnerability analysis is the pinnacle of expertise in the field of cybersecurity. It represents a level of proficiency that allows security professionals to excel in identifying, assessing, and mitigating even the most complex and sophisticated vulnerabilities. This chapter will explore the journey to achieving mastery in advanced vulnerability analysis, the skills and knowledge required, and the benefits it brings. Mastery in advanced vulnerability analysis is not something that can be achieved overnight. It is a process that requires dedication, continuous learning, and hands-on experience. Those who aspire to reach this level of expertise must start with a strong foundation in cybersecurity fundamentals. This includes a deep understanding of networking, operating systems, programming languages, and security principles. A solid grasp of these fundamentals provides the essential groundwork for advanced vulnerability analysis. Once the fundamentals are in place, individuals can begin to specialize in the field of vulnerability analysis. This involves learning about various types of vulnerabilities, including common weaknesses in software, web applications, and network infrastructure. Mastery in advanced vulnerability analysis requires a deep understanding of how these vulnerabilities can be exploited by attackers and how to defend against them. One of the key skills that advanced vulnerability analysts must develop is the ability to think like an attacker. This involves understanding the tactics, techniques, and procedures that malicious actors use to exploit vulnerabilities. By gaining insight into the mindset of attackers, analysts can better anticipate and defend against emerging threats. To achieve mastery in advanced vulnerability analysis, individuals must also become proficient in the use of a wide range of security tools and technologies. This includes vulnerability scanning tools, penetration testing frameworks, and debugging and reverse engineering tools. Advanced analysts must know how to use these tools effectively to identify vulnerabilities, assess their impact, and develop strategies for remediation. Another critical aspect of advanced vulnerability analysis is the ability to conduct in-depth research and discovery of zero-day vulnerabilities. This involves searching for previously unknown vulnerabilities in software, hardware, or network systems. Advanced analysts must be skilled in reverse engineering and code analysis to uncover these hidden vulnerabilities. They may also engage in bug hunting programs, collaborate with security researchers, and participate in the responsible disclosure of newly discovered vulnerabilities. One of the distinguishing features of mastery in advanced vulnerability analysis is the ability to develop and execute sophisticated attack and defense strategies. This includes designing and executing complex penetration tests, red teaming exercises, and exploit development. Advanced analysts may create custom exploits, malware, or scripts to demonstrate the impact of vulnerabilities and to develop effective countermeasures. Achieving mastery also involves staying up-to-date with the latest developments in the cybersecurity landscape. This includes monitoring emerging threats, new attack techniques, and evolving security technologies. Continuous learning and professional development are essential for staying at the forefront of the field. The benefits of achieving mastery in advanced vulnerability analysis are substantial. Professionals who reach this level of expertise are in high demand by organizations seeking to protect their digital assets. They can command higher salaries and take on leadership roles in security teams. Mastery also brings a deep sense of accomplishment and the knowledge that one is contributing to the security of organizations and individuals. In summary, achieving mastery in advanced vulnerability analysis is a challenging but rewarding journey. It requires a solid foundation in cybersecurity fundamentals, a deep understanding of vulnerabilities and attack techniques, proficiency in security tools and technologies, and a commitment to continuous learning. Those who reach this level of expertise are well-equipped to defend against even the most advanced and sophisticated threats, making them valuable assets to the cybersecurity community.

Advancing your expertise in advanced vulnerability analysis is an exciting and challenging journey in the field of cybersecurity. At this stage of your career, you've already built a strong foundation in cybersecurity fundamentals and have gained valuable experience in identifying, assessing, and mitigating vulnerabilities. However, to become an expert in advanced vulnerability analysis, you'll need to further develop your skills and knowledge in several key areas. One of the crucial aspects of advancing your expertise is deepening your understanding of various types of vulnerabilities. You've likely encountered common software weaknesses, web application vulnerabilities, and network vulnerabilities, but now it's time to explore more advanced and intricate ones. This includes understanding complex vulnerabilities in areas like cryptography, virtualization, and cloud security. As you delve into these advanced vulnerability types, you'll gain a more comprehensive understanding of the ever-evolving threat landscape. Additionally, it's essential to keep up with the latest security research and trends. Cyber threats are constantly evolving, and new vulnerabilities and attack techniques emerge regularly. To stay ahead of the curve, you should regularly follow security blogs, attend conferences, and participate in industry forums. Engaging with the cybersecurity community allows you to learn from others, share your knowledge, and collaborate on cutting-edge research. Moreover, becoming an expert in advanced vulnerability analysis requires honing your ability to think like an attacker. This means going beyond identifying vulnerabilities and understanding how they can be exploited to gain unauthorized access or cause harm. By putting yourself in the shoes of malicious actors, you can anticipate their tactics, techniques, and procedures and develop more effective defenses. Part of this mindset involves mastering advanced penetration testing and ethical hacking techniques. You'll need to become proficient in conducting complex penetration tests and red teaming exercises that simulate real-world attacks. This may involve simulating sophisticated threat actors, conducting targeted attacks, and crafting custom exploits. To excel in these activities, you should be well-versed in penetration testing frameworks and tools and understand how to perform advanced privilege escalation, lateral movement, and post-exploitation activities. Advanced vulnerability analysts also delve into the world of reverse engineering and exploit development. Reverse engineering involves dissecting software, firmware, or hardware to understand its inner workings. This skill is essential for discovering hidden vulnerabilities, especially in proprietary software. By examining code and binary structures, you can uncover security flaws that are not immediately apparent. Exploit development takes this knowledge further by creating functional exploits that take advantage of vulnerabilities. This process involves crafting code that can successfully compromise a system or application, often by bypassing security measures. Developing exploits requires a deep understanding of assembly language, memory management, and vulnerability exploitation techniques. In addition to technical skills, an expert in advanced vulnerability analysis must be an effective communicator. You'll need to convey complex technical findings to both technical and non-technical stakeholders. This includes writing comprehensive reports that detail your findings, risks, and recommended mitigations. Your reports should be clear, concise, and tailored to your audience, whether it's a fellow cybersecurity expert or a C-suite executive. Furthermore, becoming an expert in advanced vulnerability analysis often means taking on a leadership role in security teams. You'll be responsible for guiding and mentoring less experienced analysts, sharing your knowledge, and helping your team stay updated on the latest threats and defensive strategies. Leadership skills, including effective communication and team management, are essential at this stage of your career. Finally, achieving expertise in advanced vulnerability analysis is not a static goal. The field of cybersecurity is dynamic and ever-changing, requiring continuous learning and adaptation. You should regularly challenge yourself with new and complex scenarios, such as advanced capture the flag (CTF) challenges, security competitions, and real-world incident response exercises. Participating in these activities will help you refine your skills and keep your expertise sharp. In summary, advancing your expertise in advanced vulnerability analysis is a rewarding journey that requires ongoing dedication and learning. It involves deepening your knowledge of various vulnerability types, staying current with cybersecurity trends, thinking like an attacker, mastering penetration testing and reverse engineering, and becoming an effective communicator and leader. By continuously honing your skills and staying committed to your professional growth, you'll be well on your way to becoming an expert in advanced vulnerability analysis.

BOOK 4
ZERO DAY UNLEASHED
EXPERT-LEVEL TACTICS FOR EXPLOITING AND
PROTECTING AGAINST SOFTWARE VULNERABILITIES

ROB BOTWRIGHT

Chapter 1: The Expert's World of Zero Day Vulnerabilities

Navigating the landscape of advanced zero-day vulnerabilities is a complex and multifaceted task that requires a deep understanding of cybersecurity principles and practices. In this chapter, we will explore the intricate world of zero-day vulnerabilities, shedding light on their significance, challenges, and the strategies required to effectively navigate this terrain. Zero-day vulnerabilities are a category of software vulnerabilities that are so named because they are exploited by attackers on the same day (or zero days) that the vulnerability becomes known to the software vendor or the public. These vulnerabilities are highly sought after by cybercriminals and nation-state actors because they offer the element of surprise and can be used to launch devastating attacks.

To navigate this landscape effectively, one must first grasp the historical significance of zero-day vulnerabilities. Understanding their evolution over time provides valuable insights into their current state and the reasons behind their prevalence in today's threat landscape. Zero-day vulnerabilities have been a part of the digital world since the early days of computing. As software and technology have advanced, so too have the methods and motivations of those seeking to exploit these vulnerabilities. By examining the history of zero days, we can gain a deeper appreciation for the challenges they pose and the need for effective countermeasures.

The software development life cycle (SDLC) plays a pivotal role in the zero-day vulnerability landscape. To navigate this terrain, it's essential to comprehend how software is developed, tested, and deployed. The SDLC encompasses various stages, from requirements gathering and design to coding, testing, and maintenance. Understanding this process helps analysts identify vulnerabilities at different points in the life cycle and assess the impact of these vulnerabilities on software security.

Navigating the software ecosystem is another critical aspect of addressing zero-day vulnerabilities. In today's interconnected world, software interacts with a vast and complex ecosystem of libraries, frameworks, and third-party components. Analyzing and securing these dependencies is crucial to prevent zero-day vulnerabilities from compromising the overall security of a system.

Exploring buffer overflows and stack smashing is a fundamental topic in advanced vulnerability analysis. These exploitation techniques are commonly used to take advantage of software vulnerabilities and gain unauthorized access to systems. Understanding how buffer overflows occur and how they can be mitigated is essential for navigating the zero-day landscape effectively.

SQL injection and cross-site scripting (XSS) are prevalent attack vectors that can lead to zero-day vulnerabilities. These web application vulnerabilities can be exploited to compromise sensitive data or execute malicious code. Navigating the landscape of advanced zero-day vulnerabilities requires a deep understanding of these attack vectors and how to defend against them effectively.

The anatomy of zero-day exploits is a topic of great importance in advanced vulnerability analysis. To navigate this landscape, it's essential to dissect zero-day exploits and understand the techniques they use to compromise systems. This knowledge enables analysts to develop better defenses and detect zero-day attacks more effectively.

Real-world implications of zero-day exploits are far-reaching and can have severe consequences for individuals, organizations, and even nations. Navigating this landscape involves considering the potential impact of zero-day vulnerabilities on confidentiality, integrity, and availability. Understanding the real-world consequences helps prioritize mitigation efforts and allocate resources effectively.

Leveraging static code analysis techniques is a proactive approach to identifying zero-day vulnerabilities before they are exploited. Static analysis tools examine source code or binary executables to identify potential weaknesses and security flaws. Navigating the landscape of advanced zero-day vulnerabilities requires proficiency in using these tools to conduct thorough code reviews and vulnerability assessments.

Dynamic code analysis and testing strategies are equally crucial for navigating the zero-day landscape. Dynamic analysis techniques involve running software in a controlled environment to identify vulnerabilities that may not be apparent through static analysis alone. This includes techniques such as fuzz testing, dynamic binary analysis, and runtime instrumentation.

Introduction to vulnerability scanning is a critical step in identifying and addressing zero-day vulnerabilities. Vulnerability scanning tools help automate the process of identifying weaknesses and misconfigurations in systems and applications. Navigating the landscape of advanced zero-day vulnerabilities involves selecting the right scanning tools and techniques for comprehensive coverage.

Selecting the right scanning tools is a nuanced process that requires considering various factors, including the type of systems and applications in use, the organization's specific security requirements, and the desired level of automation. Navigating the landscape of advanced zero-day vulnerabilities involves making informed decisions about which scanning tools will best meet these needs.

The importance of accurate reporting cannot be overstated when navigating the zero-day vulnerability landscape. Effectively communicating findings, risks, and recommended mitigations is essential for driving remediation efforts and securing systems. Navigating this terrain involves mastering the art of creating clear, concise, and actionable reports.

Documentation best practices are integral to the process of addressing zero-day vulnerabilities. Navigating this landscape involves maintaining detailed records of vulnerabilities, remediation efforts, and incident response activities. Proper documentation ensures that lessons learned are retained and can be applied to future security efforts.

Understanding the impact of zero-day vulnerabilities is essential for anyone involved in cybersecurity, from analysts to executives and policymakers. Zero-day vulnerabilities are a special breed of security flaws that represent a clear and present danger to the digital world. Their impact can be profound, affecting individuals, organizations, and even nations. To gain expert insights into this impact, it's crucial to delve into the various dimensions of zero-day vulnerabilities and their consequences.

First and foremost, zero-day vulnerabilities are coveted by malicious actors for their potential to cause significant harm. These vulnerabilities are called "zero-day" because they are exploited on the very same day they are discovered, leaving software vendors with zero days to prepare and release patches. This immediacy gives attackers a substantial advantage, enabling them to launch attacks before defenders can respond effectively.

One of the most critical impacts of zero-day vulnerabilities is their potential to compromise data confidentiality. When a zero-day exploit is unleashed, attackers can gain unauthorized access to sensitive information. This may include personal data, financial records, intellectual property, and classified government documents. The consequences of such breaches can be devastating, leading to identity theft, financial losses, and espionage.

Moreover, zero-day vulnerabilities can compromise data integrity. Attackers can manipulate or alter data within compromised systems, leading to erroneous information, loss of trust, and potentially dangerous situations. For example, tampering with financial records can have far-reaching implications, eroding trust in financial institutions and damaging the economy.

The impact of zero-day vulnerabilities extends beyond data confidentiality and integrity; it also affects system availability. These vulnerabilities can be used to launch distributed denial-of-service (DDoS) attacks, rendering critical services and infrastructure inaccessible. In cases of national security, such attacks can disrupt essential services, including emergency response systems and power grids.

Another dimension of the impact of zero-day vulnerabilities is their potential for espionage and cyber warfare. Nation-state actors often seek out and hoard these vulnerabilities to gain a strategic advantage. By exploiting zero-days, they can infiltrate the networks of other nations, steal sensitive information, and disrupt critical infrastructure. This has led to a new era of digital warfare, where the consequences are not limited to the digital realm but can spill over into the physical world.

Furthermore, zero-day vulnerabilities can have severe financial consequences for organizations. When attackers breach a company's defenses using a zero-day exploit, they can cause significant financial losses, including the cost of investigating the breach, remediating the damage, and compensating affected parties. Moreover, the damage to a company's reputation can result in lost customers and revenue.

Navigating the impact of zero-day vulnerabilities requires a proactive approach to vulnerability management. Organizations must prioritize the identification and mitigation of these vulnerabilities to reduce their exposure to potential threats. This involves maintaining an up-to-date inventory of software and systems, continuously monitoring for vulnerabilities, and rapidly applying patches and security updates when they become available.

One of the challenges in addressing the impact of zero-day vulnerabilities is the covert nature of these attacks. Because zero-days are unknown to vendors and security researchers, they are challenging to detect using traditional security tools and techniques. This makes advanced threat detection and response capabilities crucial for identifying and mitigating zero-day exploits.

Collaboration is also a key factor in mitigating the impact of zero-day vulnerabilities. Organizations, security researchers, and government agencies must share information about new vulnerabilities and threats. This collective effort can lead to more rapid identification and response to zero-day exploits, reducing their impact.

The impact of zero-day vulnerabilities is not limited to the immediate consequences of an attack. It also has long-term implications for the cybersecurity landscape. As the demand for zero-days increases, a thriving underground market has emerged, where these vulnerabilities are bought, sold, and traded for significant sums of money. This ecosystem incentivizes attackers to discover and hoard zero-days, further increasing the risk for organizations and individuals.

In summary, the impact of zero-day vulnerabilities is profound and far-reaching. These vulnerabilities pose a clear and present danger to data confidentiality, integrity, and system availability. They can lead to financial losses, espionage, and even cyber warfare. Addressing the impact of zero-day vulnerabilities requires a proactive and collaborative approach, with a focus on advanced threat detection, rapid patching, and information sharing. As the digital landscape continues to evolve, understanding and mitigating the impact of zero-day vulnerabilities will remain a critical priority for cybersecurity professionals and organizations alike.

Chapter 2: Advanced Exploitation Techniques Unveiled

In the ever-evolving landscape of cybersecurity, understanding sophisticated exploitation tactics is essential for protecting digital assets and sensitive information. These tactics represent the cutting edge of cyberattacks, where threat actors employ advanced techniques to breach defenses, infiltrate networks, and achieve their malicious objectives.

At the core of sophisticated exploitation tactics is the concept of stealth. Cybercriminals and nation-state actors alike seek to avoid detection for as long as possible, allowing them to operate within compromised systems and exfiltrate data without raising alarms. To achieve this, they employ a range of techniques designed to bypass security measures and blend into the digital environment.

One sophisticated tactic is the use of advanced malware. These malicious programs are designed to evade traditional antivirus solutions by employing polymorphic code, rootkit functionality, and other obfuscation techniques. Advanced malware can often lie dormant within a system, waiting for specific conditions or triggers before activating, making it challenging to detect.

Furthermore, attackers frequently utilize zero-day vulnerabilities, which are security flaws that are unknown to the software vendor and, therefore, lack patches or updates. By exploiting these vulnerabilities, threat actors can gain unauthorized access to systems, and since there are no available patches, defenders have no immediate recourse.

Sophisticated exploitation tactics also involve social engineering techniques that manipulate human psychology. Spear-phishing, for example, targets specific individuals or organizations with tailored messages that appear legitimate. This approach increases the likelihood of luring victims into clicking on malicious links or opening infected attachments.

Moreover, advanced attackers often employ tactics like "living off the land" or "fileless" attacks. These tactics leverage legitimate system tools and processes to carry out malicious activities, making them particularly challenging to detect. By using built-in utilities and trusted applications, attackers avoid leaving suspicious traces behind.

Another key element of sophisticated exploitation tactics is lateral movement. Once inside a network, attackers seek to escalate privileges and move laterally to gain access to critical systems and data. They often exploit vulnerabilities in unpatched or misconfigured systems to move stealthily and maintain persistence.

Privilege escalation is a common tactic used by sophisticated attackers. By gaining higher-level permissions within a compromised system or network, they can access sensitive data, install additional malware, and potentially take control of critical infrastructure components. This tactic allows attackers to maximize the damage they can inflict.

Sophisticated attackers also engage in "island hopping," where they pivot from their initial target to compromise interconnected organizations or supply chain partners. This tactic can have far-reaching consequences, as it allows attackers to infiltrate multiple entities and extend their sphere of influence.

Another aspect of sophisticated exploitation tactics involves "living off the land" in the cloud. As organizations increasingly adopt cloud-based services and infrastructure, attackers have adapted by leveraging these platforms. They use legitimate cloud services to host malicious payloads, making it difficult for traditional security solutions to detect and block their activities.

Furthermore, advanced exploitation tactics often involve "fileless" attacks, which execute malicious code directly in memory without leaving a trace on the file system. This technique is difficult to detect because it relies on trusted system processes, making it a preferred choice for stealthy attackers.

In response to these sophisticated exploitation tactics, organizations and security professionals must adopt a multi-layered defense approach. This includes continuous monitoring for unusual behavior, leveraging advanced threat detection solutions, and maintaining up-to-date patches and security updates. User education and awareness are also crucial in mitigating social engineering attacks.

Moreover, organizations should implement robust access controls and privilege management to limit lateral movement within their networks. Regular penetration testing and red team exercises can help identify vulnerabilities and weaknesses in defenses, allowing for proactive remediation.

Collaboration and information sharing within the cybersecurity community are vital for staying ahead of sophisticated exploitation tactics. Threat intelligence feeds, industry partnerships, and coordinated incident response efforts can provide valuable insights and early warnings of emerging threats.

In summary, understanding and defending against sophisticated exploitation tactics are paramount in today's digital landscape. Threat actors continuously evolve their methods to bypass defenses and achieve their objectives. By staying informed, adopting advanced security measures, and fostering collaboration, organizations and security professionals can effectively counter these tactics and safeguard their digital assets.

In the world of cybersecurity, mastering the art of advanced exploitation is akin to becoming a virtuoso musician in the realm of digital threats and vulnerabilities. It is a journey that requires not only technical expertise but also creative problem-solving, persistence, and an unwavering commitment to securing the digital landscape.

Advanced exploitation is the pinnacle of offensive cybersecurity, where individuals or groups, often referred to as ethical hackers or penetration testers, harness their skills to identify and exploit vulnerabilities in computer systems, networks, and applications. This practice is an essential part of cybersecurity as it helps organizations identify weaknesses in their defenses before malicious actors can exploit them.

At its core, advanced exploitation involves understanding the intricate workings of computer systems and the myriad ways in which they can be compromised. This includes a deep knowledge of operating systems, software applications, network protocols, and hardware components. However, technical prowess alone is not enough; an ethical hacker must also possess a hacker's mindset—an innate curiosity and a relentless desire to uncover vulnerabilities.

One of the fundamental principles of advanced exploitation is the concept of "thinking like an attacker." Ethical hackers must adopt the perspective of malicious actors to anticipate their moves and stay one step ahead. This mindset enables them to identify and mitigate vulnerabilities before they can be exploited by cybercriminals.

Advanced exploitation techniques often begin with reconnaissance and information gathering. Ethical hackers scour the internet, social media, and public records to collect data about their target, such as IP addresses, domain names, employee names, and email addresses. This information forms the foundation for crafting highly targeted attacks.

With reconnaissance completed, the next phase is vulnerability scanning and enumeration. Ethical hackers use specialized tools and techniques to identify weaknesses in the target's digital infrastructure. This may involve scanning for open ports, identifying services running on those ports, and probing for known vulnerabilities.

Once vulnerabilities are identified, ethical hackers proceed to exploit them. This is where their technical expertise truly shines. Exploitation may involve crafting custom malware or leveraging existing exploits to gain unauthorized access to a system or network. The goal is to demonstrate the impact of a successful attack, often by gaining administrative or root-level access.

In advanced exploitation, it's essential to stay up-to-date with the latest vulnerabilities and exploits. This means closely following security news, monitoring vulnerability databases, and participating in the broader cybersecurity community. Zero-day vulnerabilities, which are unknown to the software vendor and have no patches available, are particularly valuable for advanced exploitation but also require a deep understanding of reverse engineering and exploit development.

Ethical hackers also use various evasion techniques to avoid detection during their activities. This includes techniques like obfuscating code, encrypting communications, and disguising their digital fingerprints. By flying under the radar, they can operate covertly within a target environment.

Persistence is a hallmark of advanced exploitation. Ethical hackers often encounter resistance in the form of robust security measures, intrusion detection systems, and skilled defenders. They must be prepared to adapt their tactics, techniques, and procedures

(TTPs) continually. This adaptability is a key differentiator between novice and advanced hackers.

Another critical aspect of mastering advanced exploitation is post-exploitation. Once access is gained, ethical hackers strive to maintain persistence within a compromised system or network. This may involve planting backdoors, creating stealthy user accounts, or hiding malicious code in unexpected places. Post-exploitation activities aim to ensure that even if the initial vulnerability is patched, the attacker can maintain access.

Beyond technical skills, advanced exploitation also demands a high degree of ethics and responsibility. Ethical hackers are bound by strict codes of conduct that prioritize the protection of systems and data. They must obtain proper authorization before conducting penetration tests, respect the confidentiality of sensitive information, and adhere to legal and regulatory requirements.

To hone their skills, ethical hackers engage in continuous learning and hands-on practice. They may participate in Capture The Flag (CTF) competitions, cybersecurity challenges, and real-world penetration tests. Many ethical hackers also pursue industry certifications like Certified Ethical Hacker (CEH), Offensive Security Certified Professional (OSCP), and Certified Information Systems Security Professional (CISSP).

Ultimately, mastering the art of advanced exploitation is a lifelong journey. It requires dedication, passion, and a commitment to the ever-evolving field of cybersecurity.

Ethical hackers play a vital role in securing the digital world, and their expertise is in high demand as organizations strive to protect their assets from increasingly sophisticated cyber threats.

In summary, advanced exploitation is a multifaceted discipline that combines technical prowess, creativity, and ethical responsibility. Ethical hackers who master this art are at the forefront of cybersecurity, helping organizations identify and mitigate vulnerabilities before malicious actors can exploit them. It is a challenging but rewarding path that requires continuous learning and a commitment to securing the digital landscape.

Chapter 3: Expert Strategies for Zero Day Discovery and Research

Exploring the realm of advanced approaches to zero-day discovery delves into the cutting-edge strategies and techniques that cybersecurity researchers employ to identify vulnerabilities before malicious actors can exploit them. This chapter will take you on a journey through the intricate and dynamic world of zero-day vulnerabilities, where knowledge, innovation, and relentless dedication are essential.

Zero-day vulnerabilities, also known as 0-days, are software flaws or weaknesses that are unknown to the vendor and have no official patches available. These vulnerabilities are prized possessions of both ethical hackers and malicious actors because they provide a unique opportunity to exploit systems, applications, or devices without the possibility of immediate remediation.

The first step in advanced zero-day discovery is understanding the software landscape. Researchers need to be intimately familiar with the target software, its architecture, and its codebase. This deep understanding allows them to identify potential weak points and areas where vulnerabilities may lurk.

Advanced researchers often take a proactive approach to zero-day discovery by focusing on specific software types or industries. For example, they might specialize in discovering vulnerabilities in web browsers, IoT devices, or critical infrastructure systems. This specialization enables them to develop domain expertise and stay ahead of emerging threats.

Advanced zero-day discovery often involves reverse engineering, a process in which researchers dissect and analyze software binaries or firmware to uncover vulnerabilities. Reverse engineering can reveal hidden flaws and security weaknesses that are not apparent through traditional code review methods.

Another critical aspect of zero-day discovery is vulnerability research. This entails actively searching for vulnerabilities in software, which can involve analyzing source code, testing software in controlled environments, and investigating crash reports and error messages. Advanced researchers often automate these processes to scale their efforts.

Open-source software plays a significant role in zero-day discovery. Researchers frequently analyze open-source projects and libraries for vulnerabilities that may have been overlooked. By contributing to the security of open-source software, they help protect a wide range of systems and applications.

Collaboration is a cornerstone of advanced zero-day discovery. Researchers often work together, sharing information, tools, and techniques to accelerate the identification of vulnerabilities. Online forums, mailing lists, and conferences provide opportunities for knowledge exchange and networking within the cybersecurity community. Advanced researchers also keep a close watch on bug bounty programs and vulnerability disclosure platforms. These programs offer financial incentives for discovering and responsibly disclosing security vulnerabilities. Engaging with bug bounty programs can be lucrative and can help advance the state of cybersecurity.

In the world of advanced zero-day discovery, creativity is a valuable asset. Researchers must think outside the box, approaching problems from unique angles and devising novel methods for identifying vulnerabilities. Sometimes, vulnerabilities are discovered through sheer serendipity or by applying unconventional techniques. The responsible disclosure of zero-day vulnerabilities is a critical ethical consideration. Advanced researchers must balance the need to protect users and systems with the potential risks of disclosing a vulnerability prematurely. They often work closely with vendors to coordinate the release of patches and advisories to minimize the impact on users.

A growing trend in advanced zero-day discovery is the use of machine learning and artificial intelligence. These technologies can analyze vast amounts of code and data to identify patterns and anomalies that might indicate the presence of vulnerabilities. Machine learning models can help researchers prioritize their efforts and focus on the most likely targets.

While zero-day vulnerabilities pose a significant threat, advanced researchers play a pivotal role in enhancing cybersecurity by uncovering and mitigating these risks. Their expertise, dedication, and innovative approaches are essential in a world where cyber threats are constantly evolving.

In summary, advanced approaches to zero-day discovery involve in-depth knowledge, proactive research, collaboration, and innovative techniques. Researchers specializing in this field navigate a complex and ever-changing landscape to identify vulnerabilities before they can be exploited by malicious actors. Their work is crucial in safeguarding the digital world and staying one step ahead of emerging cyber threats.

Chapter 4: Cutting-Edge Vulnerability Assessment Tools

In the realm of cybersecurity, staying one step ahead of threats is paramount, and leveraging state-of-the-art vulnerability assessment solutions is a cornerstone of proactive defense. These solutions are instrumental in identifying weaknesses in software, networks, and systems, providing organizations with the crucial insights needed to fortify their digital fortresses against potential attacks. At the heart of these state-of-the-art solutions are vulnerability scanners, sophisticated tools that systematically examine systems and applications for known security vulnerabilities.

These scanners are equipped with extensive databases of known vulnerabilities, which they use to compare against the target systems to determine if any weaknesses exist. One of the key advantages of modern vulnerability assessment solutions is their ability to conduct both active and passive scans.

Active scans involve sending requests to target systems and analyzing their responses to detect vulnerabilities actively. In contrast, passive scans gather information without interacting directly with the target, reducing the potential impact on live systems.

These solutions often support a wide range of scanning profiles, allowing organizations to tailor their assessments to meet specific needs.

For example, they can conduct internal scans within their network boundaries or external scans to assess internet-facing assets.

Furthermore, these solutions offer customization options to prioritize scans based on risk profiles, ensuring that critical vulnerabilities are addressed promptly.

Additionally, they can scan various types of assets, including servers, workstations, network devices, and web applications.

Automated vulnerability scanning is a hallmark of these state-of-the-art solutions, enabling organizations to assess their security posture efficiently and consistently.

By automating the scanning process, organizations can perform regular assessments, ensuring that new vulnerabilities are promptly identified.

Another significant advantage is the continuous monitoring capabilities offered by these solutions, allowing organizations to detect and remediate vulnerabilities in real-time.

In the ever-evolving landscape of cybersecurity threats, timely detection and remediation are essential to maintaining a robust defense.

Advanced vulnerability assessment solutions often provide integration capabilities with security information and event management (SIEM) systems, allowing organizations to correlate vulnerability data with other security information for a holistic view of their security posture.

Chapter 5: Offensive and Defensive Tactics in Zero Day Exploitation

The data generated by these solutions is often presented through user-friendly dashboards and reports, enabling security teams to analyze and prioritize vulnerabilities effectively.

These dashboards offer visual representations of vulnerabilities, making it easier to identify trends, patterns, and critical issues.

Furthermore, organizations can schedule automated scans, ensuring that assessments align with their security policies and compliance requirements.

Vulnerability databases, a core component of these solutions, are regularly updated with the latest threat intelligence, ensuring that organizations can identify vulnerabilities associated with emerging threats.

State-of-the-art solutions also offer advanced reporting features, allowing organizations to generate detailed reports that can be shared with stakeholders, auditors, and regulatory bodies.

These reports often include remediation recommendations and risk assessments, helping organizations prioritize their efforts to address vulnerabilities.

In addition to identifying known vulnerabilities, these solutions often include capabilities for identifying zero-day vulnerabilities—previously unknown weaknesses that have not yet been addressed by software vendors.

Advanced machine learning and artificial intelligence algorithms are increasingly integrated into these solutions, enabling more accurate and efficient vulnerability detection.

Machine learning models can analyze vast amounts of data to identify patterns and anomalies, potentially uncovering vulnerabilities that traditional methods might miss.

Moreover, these state-of-the-art solutions incorporate risk scoring mechanisms to prioritize vulnerabilities based on their potential impact and exploitability.

By focusing on high-risk vulnerabilities first, organizations can allocate resources effectively to address the most critical security issues.

Furthermore, these solutions often include capabilities for authenticated scanning, which allows organizations to assess vulnerabilities from the perspective of an authenticated user or administrator.

This type of scanning provides a comprehensive view of the vulnerabilities that could be exploited by insiders or malicious actors who gain access to privileged accounts.

State-of-the-art vulnerability assessment solutions are not limited to scanning for vulnerabilities in software and systems.

They often include web application scanning capabilities, enabling organizations to identify vulnerabilities in their web applications.

These scans can uncover issues such as SQL injection, cross-site scripting (XSS), and other web-related vulnerabilities that are often targeted by attackers.

Additionally, some solutions offer container security scanning, which is crucial in modern containerized and microservices environments.

These scans assess the security of container images, helping organizations identify vulnerabilities before they are deployed into production.

Integration with the development lifecycle is another key feature of these solutions.

By incorporating vulnerability assessments into the development and DevOps processes, organizations can identify and address vulnerabilities early in the software development lifecycle, reducing the cost and effort required for remediation.

Ultimately, leveraging state-of-the-art vulnerability assessment solutions is a proactive and essential strategy in today's cybersecurity landscape.

These solutions empower organizations to identify and remediate vulnerabilities effectively, reduce security risks, and maintain a robust defense against evolving threats.

As cyber threats continue to evolve, organizations must embrace the latest technologies and practices to protect their digital assets and maintain the trust of their   stakeholders.

In the ever-evolving landscape of cybersecurity, offensive techniques in zero-day exploitation have become increasingly sophisticated and effective.

These advanced techniques are often employed by skilled attackers to target vulnerabilities that are unknown to software vendors or security professionals.

Zero-day vulnerabilities are highly sought after by both cybercriminals and nation-state actors due to their potential to bypass traditional security measures.

Understanding these advanced offensive techniques is crucial for cybersecurity professionals tasked with defending against such threats.

One of the key principles in advanced offensive techniques is the concept of weaponizing a zero-day vulnerability.

Weaponization involves creating an exploit or a piece of malicious code that can take advantage of the specific vulnerability in a target system or application.

This process requires in-depth knowledge of the target environment, including the operating system, software, and architecture.

Attackers may use various programming languages, such as C, C++, or assembly language, to craft their exploits efficiently.

Another critical aspect of offensive techniques is the development of sophisticated payloads that can be delivered through the exploited vulnerability.

Payloads are the malicious actions or code that attackers execute on the compromised system.

These can include commands to gain unauthorized access, steal data, or establish persistent backdoors for future access.

Crafting payloads that evade detection by security solutions is a constant cat-and-mouse game between attackers and defenders.

To further enhance their offensive capabilities, attackers often employ techniques such as obfuscation and encryption to hide their malicious code from security scanners.

Obfuscation involves altering the code to make it more challenging for security tools to analyze or detect.

Encryption, on the other hand, encrypts the payload to prevent it from being detected in transit.

Attackers may also use steganography, a technique that hides malicious code within seemingly innocent files or images, making detection even more challenging.

Social engineering plays a crucial role in many advanced zero-day exploitation techniques.

Attackers often manipulate human psychology to deceive individuals into taking actions that compromise security.

These tactics can include phishing emails, where attackers send convincing but fraudulent messages to trick recipients into revealing sensitive information or clicking on malicious links.

Advanced spear-phishing campaigns target specific individuals or organizations with highly tailored messages, making them even more convincing.

Furthermore, attackers may employ zero-day vulnerabilities in popular software applications, such as web browsers or document readers, to deliver their exploits.

These attacks are known as "drive-by downloads" and require no user interaction beyond visiting a compromised website.

To evade detection, attackers may use advanced evasion techniques to bypass security controls.

These techniques manipulate the data sent to the target system in a way that security solutions cannot detect the malicious intent.

This cat-and-mouse game often leads to the development of more advanced detection and prevention methods by cybersecurity professionals.

Exploiting zero-day vulnerabilities is not limited to gaining unauthorized access to systems.

Attackers also exploit these vulnerabilities to escalate privileges within compromised systems.

Privilege escalation allows attackers to gain higher-level permissions, providing them with more control over the compromised system and potentially enabling them to move laterally within a network.

In advanced scenarios, attackers may chain multiple vulnerabilities together to achieve their goals.

This could involve exploiting one zero-day vulnerability to gain initial access and then using another to escalate privileges and maintain persistence.

In response to these advanced offensive techniques, defenders must adopt equally sophisticated defensive strategies.

This includes the implementation of advanced intrusion detection and prevention systems, which can identify and block malicious activities based on behavioral analysis and anomaly detection.

Regularly patching and updating software is essential, as it reduces the attack surface and eliminates known vulnerabilities.

Network segmentation and strict access controls can limit the lateral movement of attackers within a network, making it more challenging for them to achieve their objectives.

Advanced threat hunting and incident response capabilities are also crucial for identifying and mitigating attacks that employ zero-day vulnerabilities.

Moreover, organizations should invest in security awareness training to educate employees about the risks of social engineering and phishing attacks.

Collaboration with industry peers and information sharing through threat intelligence sharing platforms can provide valuable insights into emerging threats and advanced offensive techniques.

In summary, advanced offensive techniques in zero-day exploitation pose a significant threat in the ever-changing landscape of cybersecurity.

Understanding these techniques is essential for cybersecurity professionals to develop effective defensive strategies and stay one step ahead of attackers.

By continuously evolving their defenses and sharing threat intelligence, organizations can better protect their digital assets and networks from the advanced tactics employed by skilled adversaries.

Chapter 6: Expert-Level Vulnerability Reporting and Documentation

In the ever-evolving landscape of cybersecurity, expert defensive strategies against zero-day attacks are essential to protect organizations and their sensitive data.

These attacks, which exploit previously unknown vulnerabilities, can be incredibly challenging to defend against.

One fundamental strategy is to maintain an up-to-date inventory of all software and systems within an organization.

This inventory provides visibility into the attack surface, allowing security teams to identify and prioritize potential targets for attackers.

Regularly scanning the network for vulnerabilities and using vulnerability management tools can help discover and patch known vulnerabilities before they can be exploited.

Furthermore, organizations should employ advanced intrusion detection systems that can analyze network traffic and system behavior to identify anomalous patterns associated with zero-day attacks.

These systems often use machine learning and behavioral analysis to detect deviations from normal activity, which may indicate a zero-day exploit.

Implementing strong access controls and network segmentation is crucial for limiting the lateral movement of attackers.

By restricting access to sensitive resources and segmenting the network into isolated zones, organizations can contain and isolate potential breaches, making it more challenging for attackers to move freely within the network.

Security teams should also focus on timely and effective incident response.

This includes developing incident response plans, conducting regular tabletop exercises, and ensuring that the team is well-prepared to respond to zero-day attacks when they occur.

Collaboration with external security organizations and industry peers can provide valuable threat intelligence and insights into emerging zero-day vulnerabilities and attack techniques.

Engaging with organizations that share threat intelligence and being part of information-sharing communities can help security teams stay informed and prepared.

Moreover, organizations should prioritize employee cybersecurity training to raise awareness about social engineering and phishing attacks, which are common vectors for zero-day exploits.

Employees play a critical role in identifying and reporting suspicious activities, and a well-informed workforce can act as an additional layer of defense.

Another important aspect of defensive strategies against zero-day attacks is monitoring for unusual or unexpected behaviors within the network.

Security information and event management (SIEM) systems can help aggregate and correlate data from various sources, providing insights into potential threats and anomalies.

By proactively monitoring the network for signs of compromise, organizations can detect and respond to zero-day attacks more rapidly.

Regularly updating and patching software is a fundamental defensive measure against known vulnerabilities that attackers may attempt to exploit.

Although zero-day attacks target unknown vulnerabilities, maintaining a robust patch management process can significantly reduce the attack surface.

Organizations should also consider the use of deception technologies, such as honeypots and honeynets, which can lure attackers into environments designed for monitoring and analysis.

Deception technologies can help security teams gather valuable threat intelligence and detect zero-day attacks by enticing attackers to interact with decoy systems.

Intrusion prevention systems (IPS) that utilize threat intelligence feeds can help identify and block known malicious indicators.

By leveraging up-to-date threat intelligence, IPS solutions can prevent attackers from using known attack patterns and malware to exploit zero-day vulnerabilities.

Furthermore, endpoint detection and response (EDR) solutions can provide granular visibility into endpoint activities and behaviors.

These solutions allow security teams to monitor and respond to suspicious activities, even when dealing with unknown or zero-day threats.

Continuous security monitoring and threat hunting efforts are crucial components of a robust defensive strategy.

Security teams should actively search for indicators of compromise and signs of advanced attacks within the network.

Employing machine learning and artificial intelligence (AI) for threat detection can enhance an organization's ability to identify zero-day attacks by recognizing patterns and behaviors indicative of malicious activity.

Additionally, organizations should invest in threat intelligence platforms that provide real-time information about emerging threats, including zero-day vulnerabilities and exploits.

These platforms enable security teams to stay informed about the latest threats and adjust their defensive strategies accordingly.

Ultimately, expert defensive strategies against zero-day attacks require a multi-layered approach that encompasses technology, processes, and human resources.

By staying vigilant, proactive, and well-prepared, organizations can significantly reduce the risk posed by these advanced and elusive threats.

While there is no foolproof defense against zero-day attacks, a combination of the aforementioned strategies can greatly enhance an organization's ability to detect, mitigate, and respond to these challenging security threats.

Chapter 7: Proactive and Reactive Expert Remediation Strategies

Advanced techniques in vulnerability reporting are essential for security professionals, as they play a crucial role in the identification, mitigation, and remediation of security vulnerabilities.

These techniques go beyond basic reporting and involve a more comprehensive and strategic approach.

One key aspect of advanced vulnerability reporting is understanding the importance of context.

Security professionals should not merely report a vulnerability but provide context about its potential impact on the organization.

This includes assessing the severity of the vulnerability, the likelihood of exploitation, and the potential business consequences.

By providing context, security teams help stakeholders make informed decisions about prioritizing and addressing vulnerabilities.

Another critical element is clear and concise documentation.

In advanced reporting, it's vital to document vulnerabilities in a structured and detailed manner.

This documentation should include information about the affected systems, the specific vulnerabilities identified, and any potential attack vectors.

Additionally, reporting should provide clear steps for remediation or mitigation.

Well-documented reports streamline the resolution process and facilitate communication between security teams and other stakeholders.

Collaboration is a fundamental aspect of advanced vulnerability reporting.

Security professionals should work closely with various teams within an organization, including IT, development, and compliance, to ensure that vulnerabilities are addressed effectively.

Collaboration allows for a holistic approach to vulnerability management, ensuring that all relevant parties are involved in the remediation process.

Incorporating risk assessment into vulnerability reporting is another advanced technique.

Security professionals should assess the risk associated with each vulnerability, taking into account the potential impact on the organization.

This assessment should consider factors such as the criticality of the affected system, the sensitivity of the data involved, and the likelihood of exploitation.

By quantifying risk, organizations can prioritize vulnerabilities and allocate resources accordingly.

Advanced reporting also involves the use of specialized tools and automation.

Security teams can leverage vulnerability scanning and assessment tools to identify and report vulnerabilities more efficiently.

These tools provide in-depth analysis and help prioritize vulnerabilities based on their severity and potential impact.

Automation can streamline the reporting process by generating reports and alerts, allowing security professionals to focus on more complex tasks.

Incorporating threat intelligence into vulnerability reporting is another advanced technique.

By staying informed about the latest threats and attack techniques, security professionals can provide valuable context in their reports.

Threat intelligence helps organizations understand the evolving threat landscape and how vulnerabilities may be exploited by malicious actors.

Furthermore, vulnerability reporting should consider the broader security posture of the organization.

Security professionals should not view vulnerabilities in isolation but as part of the overall security landscape.

Reports should highlight how vulnerabilities may be interconnected and how their exploitation could lead to broader security breaches.

Additionally, advanced vulnerability reporting should align with industry standards and compliance requirements.

Security professionals should be well-versed in relevant regulations and standards, such as GDPR, HIPAA, or NIST, and ensure that vulnerability reporting complies with these frameworks.

This alignment helps organizations maintain regulatory compliance while addressing vulnerabilities.

Furthermore, advanced reporting involves continuous monitoring and tracking of vulnerabilities.

Security teams should not consider reporting a one-time activity but an ongoing process.

Regularly revisiting and updating vulnerability reports ensures that they remain relevant and reflect the changing threat landscape.

Vulnerability reporting should also consider the potential for zero-day vulnerabilities.

While advanced techniques focus on known vulnerabilities, it's essential to be prepared for the discovery of zero-day vulnerabilities that have no available patches.

Reporting such vulnerabilities requires careful coordination and communication with vendors, security researchers, and relevant authorities.

Moreover, security professionals should be aware of responsible disclosure practices.

Advanced vulnerability reporting involves ethical considerations.

Security researchers must follow responsible disclosure practices, which include notifying vendors and allowing them time to develop and release patches before disclosing the vulnerability publicly.

This responsible approach helps protect users and organizations while fostering positive collaboration within the security community.

Finally, advanced vulnerability reporting should incorporate lessons learned from previous incidents and vulnerabilities.

Security teams should conduct post-incident reviews to analyze how vulnerabilities were handled and what improvements can be made.

These reviews help organizations refine their vulnerability reporting processes and enhance their overall security posture.

In summary, advanced techniques in vulnerability reporting go beyond the basics and involve a comprehensive and strategic approach to identifying, documenting, and mitigating security vulnerabilities.

These techniques encompass providing context, clear documentation, collaboration, risk assessment, the use of specialized tools, incorporating threat intelligence, considering the broader security landscape, aligning with industry standards, continuous monitoring, and responsible disclosure.

By adopting these advanced techniques, organizations can enhance their vulnerability management practices and better protect their systems and data.

Advanced remediation approaches are a critical component of proactive protection in the ever-evolving landscape of cybersecurity.

These approaches build upon the foundation of traditional remediation strategies to address complex and emerging threats.

Next, we will delve into advanced remediation techniques that organizations can adopt to bolster their security posture.

One of the fundamental principles of advanced remediation is the need for a proactive mindset.

Instead of waiting for security incidents to occur, organizations should anticipate potential vulnerabilities and threats and take preemptive measures to mitigate them.

This proactive approach involves continuously monitoring the IT environment for signs of vulnerabilities and proactively addressing them.

Advanced remediation also involves the concept of threat hunting.

This is a proactive practice where security teams actively seek out signs of malicious activity or vulnerabilities within the organization's network.

Threat hunters use a combination of tools, techniques, and expertise to identify potential threats that may have gone unnoticed by traditional security measures.

By actively seeking out threats, organizations can discover and remediate vulnerabilities before they are exploited.

Another key aspect of advanced remediation is the use of machine learning and artificial intelligence (AI) technologies.

These technologies enable security teams to analyze vast amounts of data and identify patterns and anomalies that may indicate security threats or vulnerabilities.

Machine learning algorithms can detect unusual behavior in real-time and trigger automated responses to mitigate threats.

Machine learning and AI are particularly valuable for identifying zero-day vulnerabilities and advanced persistent threats (APTs).

Advanced remediation also involves the concept of predictive analysis.

Predictive analysis uses historical data, machine learning, and statistical modeling to predict future security threats and vulnerabilities.

By analyzing past incidents and trends, organizations can identify patterns that may indicate potential future attacks.

This allows them to proactively implement security measures to prevent these threats from materializing.

Additionally, advanced remediation techniques include the use of threat intelligence feeds.

These feeds provide organizations with real-time information about emerging threats, vulnerabilities, and attack techniques.

Security teams can use threat intelligence to stay informed about the latest threats and adapt their remediation strategies accordingly.

Furthermore, organizations should consider leveraging security orchestration, automation, and response (SOAR) solutions.

SOAR platforms enable security teams to automate the detection and response to security incidents.

They can create playbooks that define specific actions to be taken in response to different types of threats.

This automation not only accelerates incident response but also ensures consistency and accuracy in remediation efforts.

Moreover, advanced remediation techniques incorporate the concept of continuous improvement.

Security teams should regularly review and update their remediation strategies based on lessons learned from previous incidents and emerging threats.

This iterative approach ensures that remediation efforts remain effective and adaptable to evolving threats.

Incorporating a threat-centric mindset is essential for advanced remediation.

Rather than focusing solely on vulnerabilities, organizations should consider the tactics, techniques, and procedures (TTPs) used by threat actors.

By understanding how adversaries operate, organizations can design remediation strategies that target the root causes of security threats.

Additionally, organizations should adopt a comprehensive and integrated approach to security.

This involves aligning remediation efforts with other security functions, such as threat detection, incident response, and vulnerability management.

A holistic approach ensures that remediation is part of a larger security ecosystem that works together seamlessly to protect the organization.

Furthermore, advanced remediation includes the concept of continuous monitoring.

This means that security teams should continuously monitor their IT environment for signs of vulnerabilities, threats, and breaches.

Continuous monitoring allows organizations to detect and respond to security incidents in real-time, minimizing the impact of breaches.

Advanced remediation techniques also encompass the concept of security resilience.

Security resilience involves designing systems and processes to withstand and recover from security incidents.

This means that organizations should have backup and recovery plans in place to ensure business continuity in the event of a breach.

Additionally, organizations should regularly test their resilience measures to ensure they are effective.

Lastly, advanced remediation should be underpinned by a strong incident response plan.

Organizations should have a well-defined incident response plan in place that outlines the steps to be taken in the event of a security incident.

This plan should include procedures for containing the incident, investigating the breach, remediating vulnerabilities, and communicating with stakeholders.

In summary, advanced remediation approaches are essential for proactive protection in today's complex cybersecurity landscape.

These approaches involve a proactive mindset, threat hunting, the use of machine learning and AI, predictive analysis, threat intelligence feeds, SOAR solutions, continuous improvement, a threat-centric mindset, a comprehensive and integrated approach, continuous monitoring, security resilience, and a robust incident response plan.

By adopting advanced remediation techniques, organizations can better protect their systems and data from emerging threats and vulnerabilities.

Chapter 8: Expert Security Practices and Threat Mitigation

In the world of cybersecurity, where threats are constantly evolving and becoming more sophisticated, advanced security practices for experts are paramount.

These practices are designed for seasoned professionals who have a deep understanding of cybersecurity principles and want to take their skills to the next level.

One of the fundamental aspects of advanced security practices is threat modeling.

Experts should be adept at analyzing their organization's assets, identifying potential threats, and evaluating the impact and likelihood of those threats.

By conducting thorough threat modeling exercises, experts can prioritize security measures effectively.

Furthermore, experts should be well-versed in the principles of least privilege and zero trust.

Least privilege restricts user and system access rights to the minimum levels required to perform their job functions, reducing the attack surface.

Zero trust is a security model that trusts no one, not even users within the organization's network, and requires constant verification of identity and security posture.

Advanced experts understand how to implement these principles to enhance security.

Another critical aspect of advanced security practices is continuous monitoring and threat detection.

Experts should utilize advanced tools and technologies to continuously monitor their organization's network for signs of malicious activity.

This includes the use of intrusion detection systems (IDS), intrusion prevention systems (IPS), security information and event management (SIEM) solutions, and advanced threat intelligence feeds.

Moreover, experts should be skilled in the art of penetration testing.

Penetration testing, also known as ethical hacking, involves simulating cyberattacks to identify vulnerabilities in an organization's systems.

Advanced experts can conduct penetration tests with a high degree of sophistication, emulating real-world attack scenarios and providing actionable insights for remediation.

Advanced security practices also encompass secure coding and application security.

Experts should have a deep understanding of secure coding practices to identify and remediate vulnerabilities in software applications.

This includes knowledge of common vulnerabilities like SQL injection, cross-site scripting (XSS), and buffer overflows, as well as techniques to mitigate them.

Furthermore, experts should be well-versed in secure software development lifecycles (SDLC) to ensure security is integrated from the beginning of the development process.

In addition to secure coding, advanced experts should be skilled in cloud security.

With the widespread adoption of cloud computing, securing cloud environments is crucial.

Experts should understand cloud security best practices, including identity and access management (IAM), data encryption, and secure configuration of cloud services.

Moreover, advanced experts should have expertise in threat hunting and incident response.

Threat hunting involves actively searching for signs of malicious activity within an organization's network, even when there are no known indicators of compromise.

Advanced experts can use their experience to uncover hidden threats and vulnerabilities.

When an incident occurs, experts should be well-prepared to respond effectively.

This includes containment, eradication, and recovery procedures, as well as legal and regulatory considerations.

Advanced security practices also extend to the realm of network security.

Experts should have a deep understanding of network protocols, traffic analysis, and advanced firewall configurations to protect against sophisticated attacks.

Additionally, experts should be familiar with security information sharing and analysis centers (ISACs) and information sharing and analysis organizations (ISAOs) to stay informed about emerging threats and vulnerabilities.

Furthermore, experts should be well-versed in security automation and orchestration.

Automation can streamline routine security tasks, allowing experts to focus on more complex and strategic aspects of cybersecurity.

Advanced experts can design and implement automated workflows that respond to security incidents in real-time.

Moreover, advanced security practices include a strong emphasis on security awareness and training.

Experts should be skilled at creating and delivering effective security awareness programs to educate employees about cybersecurity risks and best practices.

This includes phishing awareness training, social engineering awareness, and secure password practices.

Additionally, experts should possess expertise in regulatory compliance and privacy.

Depending on the industry, organizations may be subject to various regulatory requirements, such as the General Data Protection Regulation (GDPR), the Health Insurance Portability and Accountability Act (HIPAA), or the Payment Card Industry Data Security Standard (PCI DSS).

Experts should understand these regulations and ensure their organization's compliance.

In the realm of endpoint security, advanced experts should be proficient in advanced endpoint detection and response (EDR) solutions.

EDR solutions provide real-time visibility into endpoint activity and enable rapid response to threats.

Advanced experts can fine-tune EDR systems to detect and respond to advanced threats effectively.

Moreover, experts should be well-versed in threat intelligence and information sharing.

By actively participating in threat intelligence communities and sharing information about emerging threats and vulnerabilities, experts contribute to the collective defense against cyberattacks.

Additionally, advanced experts should have a deep understanding of secure network architecture and segmentation.

This involves designing networks to minimize lateral movement by attackers and isolating critical assets from less secure parts of the network.

Furthermore, experts should be skilled in identity and access management (IAM).

IAM systems are essential for managing user identities, roles, and access privileges effectively.

Advanced experts can implement IAM solutions that provide granular control over user access and reduce the risk of unauthorized access.

In summary, advanced security practices for experts encompass a wide range of knowledge and skills that are essential for protecting organizations in the face of increasingly sophisticated cyber threats.

From threat modeling and zero trust principles to penetration testing, secure coding, and cloud security, advanced experts must continuously expand their expertise to stay ahead of cyber adversaries.

By mastering these advanced practices, experts can play a crucial role in safeguarding their organizations from evolving cybersecurity risks.

In the world of cybersecurity, where threats are constantly evolving and becoming more sophisticated, advanced security practices for experts are paramount. These practices are designed for seasoned professionals who have a deep understanding of cybersecurity principles and want to take their skills to the next level.

One of the fundamental aspects of advanced security practices is threat modeling.

Experts should be adept at analyzing their organization's assets, identifying potential threats, and evaluating the impact and likelihood of those threats.

By conducting thorough threat modeling exercises, experts can prioritize security measures effectively.

Furthermore, experts should be well-versed in the principles of least privilege and zero trust.

Least privilege restricts user and system access rights to the minimum levels required to perform their job functions, reducing the attack surface.

Zero trust is a security model that trusts no one, not even users within the organization's network, and requires constant verification of identity and security posture.

Advanced experts understand how to implement these principles to enhance security.

Another critical aspect of advanced security practices is continuous monitoring and threat detection.

Experts should utilize advanced tools and technologies to continuously monitor their organization's network for signs of malicious activity.

This includes the use of intrusion detection systems (IDS), intrusion prevention systems (IPS), security information and event management (SIEM) solutions, and advanced threat intelligence feeds.

Moreover, experts should be skilled in the art of penetration testing.

Penetration testing, also known as ethical hacking, involves simulating cyberattacks to identify vulnerabilities in an organization's systems.

Advanced experts can conduct penetration tests with a high degree of sophistication, emulating real-world attack scenarios and providing actionable insights for remediation.

Advanced security practices also encompass secure coding and application security.

Experts should have a deep understanding of secure coding practices to identify and remediate vulnerabilities in software applications.

This includes knowledge of common vulnerabilities like SQL injection, cross-site scripting (XSS), and buffer overflows, as well as techniques to mitigate them.

Furthermore, experts should be well-versed in secure software development lifecycles (SDLC) to ensure security is integrated from the beginning of the development process.

In addition to secure coding, advanced experts should be skilled in cloud security.

With the widespread adoption of cloud computing, securing cloud environments is crucial.

Experts should understand cloud security best practices, including identity and access management (IAM), data encryption, and secure configuration of cloud services.

Moreover, advanced experts should have expertise in threat hunting and incident response.

Threat hunting involves actively searching for signs of malicious activity within an organization's network, even when there are no known indicators of compromise.

Advanced experts can use their experience to uncover hidden threats and vulnerabilities.

When an incident occurs, experts should be well-prepared to respond effectively.

This includes containment, eradication, and recovery procedures, as well as legal and regulatory considerations.

Advanced security practices also extend to the realm of network security.

Experts should have a deep understanding of network protocols, traffic analysis, and advanced firewall configurations to protect against sophisticated attacks.

Additionally, experts should be familiar with security information sharing and analysis centers (ISACs) and information sharing and analysis organizations (ISAOs) to stay informed about emerging threats and vulnerabilities.

Furthermore, experts should be well-versed in security automation and orchestration.

Automation can streamline routine security tasks, allowing experts to focus on more complex and strategic aspects of cybersecurity.

Advanced experts can design and implement automated workflows that respond to security incidents in real-time.

Moreover, advanced security practices include a strong emphasis on security awareness and training.

Experts should be skilled at creating and delivering effective security awareness programs to educate employees about cybersecurity risks and best practices.

This includes phishing awareness training, social engineering awareness, and secure password practices.

Additionally, experts should possess expertise in regulatory compliance and privacy.

Depending on the industry, organizations may be subject to various regulatory requirements, such as the General Data Protection Regulation (GDPR), the Health Insurance Portability and Accountability Act (HIPAA), or the Payment Card Industry Data Security Standard (PCI DSS).

Experts should understand these regulations and ensure their organization's compliance.

In the realm of endpoint security, advanced experts should be proficient in advanced endpoint detection and response (EDR) solutions.

EDR solutions provide real-time visibility into endpoint activity and enable rapid response to threats.

Advanced experts can fine-tune EDR systems to detect and respond to advanced threats effectively.

Moreover, experts should be well-versed in threat intelligence and information sharing.

By actively participating in threat intelligence communities and sharing information about emerging threats and vulnerabilities, experts contribute to the collective defense against cyberattacks.

Additionally, advanced experts should have a deep understanding of secure network architecture and segmentation.

This involves designing networks to minimize lateral movement by attackers and isolating critical assets from less secure parts of the network.

Furthermore, experts should be skilled in identity and access management (IAM).

IAM systems are essential for managing user identities, roles, and access privileges effectively.

Advanced experts can implement IAM solutions that provide granular control over user access and reduce the risk of unauthorized access.

In summary, advanced security practices for experts encompass a wide range of knowledge and skills that are essential for protecting organizations in the face of increasingly sophisticated cyber threats.

From threat modeling and zero trust principles to penetration testing, secure coding, and cloud security, advanced experts must continuously expand their expertise to stay ahead of cyber adversaries.

By mastering these advanced practices, experts can play a crucial role in safeguarding their organizations from evolving cybersecurity risks.

Chapter 9: Leading Collaborative Efforts in Vulnerability Mitigation

Collaborative mitigation at the expert level is a crucial aspect of modern cybersecurity, where threats are increasingly sophisticated and require a collective defense approach.

Experts understand that no single organization can address all cybersecurity challenges on its own, and collaboration is essential to strengthen defenses.

One key element of collaborative mitigation is information sharing.

Experts actively participate in Information Sharing and Analysis Centers (ISACs) and other threat intelligence communities, where organizations share data about emerging threats and vulnerabilities.

This collective intelligence helps organizations stay ahead of attackers and adapt their defenses accordingly.

Furthermore, experts engage in collaborative threat hunting.

This involves working with other organizations, including peers in the same industry or sector, to actively search for signs of malicious activity that may be targeting multiple entities.

Sharing threat hunting techniques and findings can uncover coordinated attacks that would otherwise go unnoticed.

In addition to collaborative threat hunting, experts understand the importance of joint incident response efforts.

When a cybersecurity incident occurs, experts collaborate with other organizations to share information about the attack, the tactics used by the adversary, and the indicators of compromise.

This information exchange enables a faster and more effective response, as it provides a broader perspective on the threat.

Moreover, experts engage in collaborative red teaming exercises.

Red teaming involves simulating cyberattacks to identify vulnerabilities and weaknesses in an organization's defenses.

Experts from multiple organizations can participate in red teaming exercises to assess the collective security posture and identify areas for improvement.

Additionally, experts participate in public-private partnerships.

These partnerships involve collaboration between government agencies and private-sector organizations to enhance national and international cybersecurity.

Through these partnerships, experts contribute to the development of cybersecurity policies, regulations, and best practices that benefit the entire ecosystem.

Furthermore, experts engage in joint threat intelligence sharing.

This involves sharing intelligence about specific threats, such as advanced persistent threats (APTs) or nation-state-sponsored attacks, with trusted partners.

By sharing this specialized threat intelligence, organizations can better defend against targeted attacks.

Additionally, experts participate in coordinated vulnerability disclosure programs.

When a security researcher discovers a vulnerability, they can work with organizations to responsibly disclose the vulnerability and coordinate the release of patches or mitigations.

This collaborative approach helps protect users and organizations from potential exploitation.

Moreover, experts engage in joint cyber exercises and simulations.

These exercises involve multiple organizations simulating cyberattacks and responses to enhance their collective readiness for real-world incidents.

By practicing together, organizations can improve their incident response coordination.

Additionally, experts understand the importance of cross-sector collaboration.

Cyber threats often target multiple sectors simultaneously, such as critical infrastructure, finance, and healthcare.

Experts from different sectors collaborate to share threat intelligence and best practices for sector-specific challenges.

Furthermore, experts engage in international collaboration.

Cyber threats are not confined by national borders, and experts work with counterparts from other countries to address global cybersecurity challenges.

International cooperation is vital to combatting transnational cybercrime and state-sponsored cyberattacks.

Additionally, experts actively participate in industry-specific Information Sharing and Analysis Centers (ISACs).

These organizations bring together companies within a particular industry to share threat intelligence and collaborate on security measures tailored to their sector's unique challenges.

Moreover, experts engage in supply chain security collaboration.

They understand that vulnerabilities in the supply chain can pose significant risks, and they work with suppliers and partners to enhance supply chain security.

Collaborative risk assessments are conducted to identify potential weaknesses and implement mitigations.

Additionally, experts participate in joint threat mitigation efforts.

When a significant cyber threat emerges, experts from various organizations collaborate to mitigate the threat collectively.

This can involve sharing threat indicators, developing and distributing signatures for detection, and coordinating the removal of malicious infrastructure.

Furthermore, experts actively engage in public-private threat sharing partnerships.

These partnerships involve government agencies and private-sector organizations sharing threat intelligence to protect critical infrastructure and national security.

Experts contribute to these partnerships by providing valuable insights and intelligence.

In summary, orchestrating collaborative mitigation at the expert level is essential in the face of increasingly sophisticated cyber threats.

Experts engage in information sharing, collaborative threat hunting, joint incident response efforts, red teaming exercises, public-private partnerships, and more to enhance cybersecurity collectively.

By working together, organizations can better defend against cyber threats and adapt to the evolving threat landscape.

In the realm of advanced vulnerability mitigation, leading cross-team initiatives plays a pivotal role in safeguarding organizations from evolving cyber threats.

These initiatives are a reflection of the growing complexity of modern vulnerabilities and the need for a comprehensive, multidisciplinary approach.

Leading such efforts requires a diverse skill set and a deep understanding of both technical and organizational aspects of cybersecurity.

At its core, cross-team vulnerability mitigation revolves around collaboration among different teams and departments within an organization.

Cybersecurity teams must work hand in hand with IT, compliance, legal, and even business units to create a unified front against vulnerabilities.

The first step in leading these initiatives is to establish clear objectives.

What is the specific vulnerability or set of vulnerabilities that the organization aims to mitigate?

Are there compliance requirements or regulatory standards that need to be met?

Defining the goals of the initiative is crucial to guide subsequent actions effectively.

Moreover, it's essential to assemble a cross-functional team with the right expertise.

This team should include technical experts who understand the intricacies of the vulnerabilities in question, but also individuals who can provide legal, compliance, and communication insights.

Each team member brings a unique perspective and skill set to the table.

Once the team is in place, a comprehensive risk assessment is conducted.

This assessment involves identifying and prioritizing vulnerabilities based on factors such as their potential impact on the organization, the likelihood of exploitation, and the available resources for mitigation.

It's also essential to consider the organization's risk tolerance and business objectives when prioritizing vulnerabilities.

Next, a mitigation strategy is developed. This strategy should outline the specific steps and actions required to address each vulnerability.

It may involve implementing patches, reconfiguring systems, enhancing access controls, or even redesigning certain processes. The mitigation strategy should also address any legal or compliance considerations, ensuring that actions taken align with regulatory requirements. Communication is a critical aspect of leading cross-team vulnerability mitigation initiatives.

Clear and effective communication channels must be established among team members, stakeholders, and affected parties.

This includes providing regular updates on the progress of mitigation efforts and informing stakeholders of any potential impacts or disruptions.

Transparency and open communication are essential to maintain trust and collaboration.

Another key element is continuous monitoring.

Vulnerability landscapes are dynamic, and new threats may emerge even after initial mitigation efforts.

Regularly monitoring the security posture of the organization allows for the timely identification of new vulnerabilities and the adjustment of mitigation strategies as needed.

Moreover, leading cross-team initiatives involves fostering a culture of security awareness within the organization.

All employees should be educated about the importance of vulnerability mitigation and their role in it.

Training and awareness programs can help employees recognize and report potential vulnerabilities.

Additionally, it's crucial to conduct thorough post-mitigation assessments.

After vulnerabilities have been addressed, it's essential to evaluate the effectiveness of the mitigation efforts.

Were the identified vulnerabilities adequately addressed?

Were there any unintended consequences or side effects of the mitigation actions?

Post-mitigation assessments provide valuable insights for refining future vulnerability mitigation initiatives.

Furthermore, it's important to document the entire process.

Detailed records should be maintained, including risk assessments, mitigation plans, communication logs, and post-mitigation assessments.

This documentation serves as a historical record and can be valuable for compliance purposes or when facing future vulnerabilities.

Leading cross-team initiatives also involves adaptability.

Cyber threats and vulnerabilities are continually evolving, and mitigation strategies must evolve as well.

The cross-functional team should remain flexible and prepared to adjust strategies and tactics based on emerging threats and changing circumstances.

Moreover, collaboration with external partners can be beneficial.

Sharing information and best practices with peers in the industry or sector can enhance vulnerability mitigation efforts.

External partnerships can provide insights into emerging threats and novel mitigation approaches.

In summary, leading cross-team initiatives for advanced vulnerability mitigation is a multifaceted endeavor that requires careful planning, collaboration, communication, and adaptability.

It involves assembling the right team, conducting thorough risk assessments, developing effective mitigation strategies, and maintaining a culture of security awareness.

Continuous monitoring, post-mitigation assessments, and documentation are crucial for ongoing improvement.

By taking a holistic approach and leveraging the expertise of various teams and departments, organizations can better protect themselves against the ever-evolving landscape of cyber threats.

Chapter 10: Mastering Expert-Level Vulnerability Analysis and Protection

In the realm of cybersecurity, achieving mastery in expert-level vulnerability analysis represents the pinnacle of knowledge and skill in identifying, assessing, and mitigating vulnerabilities.

Expert-level analysts possess a deep and nuanced understanding of the ever-evolving threat landscape, making them invaluable assets to organizations seeking to fortify their defenses against cyberattacks.

To embark on the journey toward mastery in expert-level vulnerability analysis, one must first recognize the significance of this role in the broader context of cybersecurity.

These analysts are not only tasked with identifying vulnerabilities but also with comprehensively understanding the potential impact of these vulnerabilities on an organization's security posture.

They must be well-versed in the tactics, techniques, and procedures employed by threat actors who seek to exploit vulnerabilities for malicious purposes.

Expert-level analysts are often at the forefront of safeguarding an organization's sensitive data, critical infrastructure, and reputation.

One of the key characteristics that sets expert-level analysts apart is their ability to think like attackers.

They adopt a hacker's mindset to anticipate how vulnerabilities could be exploited and the potential pathways that attackers might take.

This mindset allows them to proactively identify weaknesses before malicious actors can exploit them.

To reach this level of expertise, aspiring analysts must acquire a deep knowledge of various programming languages, operating systems, and network architectures.

They must also be proficient in using a wide array of cybersecurity tools and technologies, as well as staying updated on the latest developments in the field.

Expert-level analysts often possess industry-recognized certifications such as Certified Information Systems Security Professional (CISSP), Certified Ethical Hacker (CEH), and Certified Information Security Manager (CISM) to validate their expertise.

Beyond technical skills, expert-level vulnerability analysts excel in critical thinking and problem-solving.

They approach each vulnerability with a holistic perspective, considering its potential impact on the organization's operations, data integrity, and compliance requirements.

They also factor in the organization's unique risk tolerance and business objectives when prioritizing vulnerabilities for mitigation.

Expert-level analysts understand that vulnerability analysis is not just about identifying weaknesses but also about making informed decisions regarding which vulnerabilities pose the greatest threats.

Another hallmark of expert-level analysts is their proficiency in conducting in-depth vulnerability assessments.

These assessments go beyond automated scanning tools and involve manual testing, code analysis, and penetration testing to uncover vulnerabilities that might evade automated detection.

Expert-level analysts possess the skills to identify vulnerabilities in both software applications and the underlying infrastructure, ensuring that all potential attack vectors are considered.

Furthermore, they are adept at analyzing vulnerabilities in the context of specific threat landscapes.

They understand the motivations and capabilities of various threat actors, whether they are nation-states, criminal organizations, or hacktivists.

This knowledge allows expert-level analysts to tailor their mitigation strategies to address the most relevant and likely threats.

Collaboration is a critical aspect of expert-level vulnerability analysis.

These analysts work closely with cross-functional teams within an organization, including IT, legal, compliance, and business units.

They communicate technical findings in a clear and comprehensible manner to non-technical stakeholders, facilitating informed decision-making at all levels of the organization.

Moreover, expert-level analysts are skilled in developing and implementing comprehensive vulnerability mitigation strategies.

They recognize that mitigation involves more than just patching software; it may require changes to network configurations, access controls, and even business processes.

These analysts weigh the potential risks and benefits of different mitigation approaches and develop tailored strategies that align with the organization's goals.

In addition to their technical acumen, expert-level analysts possess a deep sense of ethical responsibility.

They adhere to strict codes of conduct and ethics, ensuring that their actions and findings do not harm the organizations they are tasked with protecting.

This ethical foundation is particularly important when conducting vulnerability research and responsible disclosure of zero-day vulnerabilities.

Mentorship and continuous learning are integral components of achieving mastery in expert-level vulnerability analysis.

Aspiring analysts often seek guidance from experienced mentors who can provide insights, share real-world experiences, and offer constructive feedback.

They also engage in ongoing training and professional development to stay ahead of emerging threats and evolving attack techniques.

Furthermore, expert-level analysts often contribute to the broader cybersecurity community through knowledge sharing, research publications, and participation in industry conferences.

Their contributions help advance the field and raise awareness of the importance of vulnerability analysis.

To summarize, achieving mastery in expert-level vulnerability analysis is a journey that requires a combination of technical expertise, critical thinking, ethical responsibility, collaboration, and continuous learning.

These analysts play a pivotal role in safeguarding organizations from cyber threats and ensuring the integrity of their digital assets.

They are proactive, adaptable, and committed to staying ahead of the ever-changing cybersecurity landscape.

In doing so, they contribute not only to the security of their organizations but also to the broader cybersecurity community.

In the realm of cybersecurity, expert techniques for protecting against advanced vulnerabilities are indispensable safeguards against the ever-evolving threat landscape.

These techniques represent the culmination of knowledge and skill, enabling organizations to fortify their defenses against the most sophisticated cyber threats.

To embark on the journey of mastering expert techniques for protecting against advanced vulnerabilities, one must first recognize the dynamic nature of modern cyberattacks.

Today's threat actors employ a myriad of tactics, techniques, and procedures to exploit vulnerabilities and infiltrate networks.

Expert practitioners understand that these adversaries are relentless and constantly adapt their methods, requiring a proactive and multi-faceted approach to defense.

One of the primary distinctions of expert-level protection techniques is their emphasis on proactive defense strategies.

Rather than merely responding to known threats, experts take a forward-looking approach, anticipating potential vulnerabilities and weaknesses in their organization's security posture.

This proactive mindset allows them to identify and mitigate vulnerabilities before they can be exploited by malicious actors.

Achieving expertise in advanced vulnerability protection begins with a comprehensive understanding of an organization's assets, data, and potential attack vectors.

Experts conduct thorough asset inventories to identify critical systems and data that require the highest level of protection.

They also map out network topologies and assess potential points of entry that attackers might exploit.

Furthermore, they categorize vulnerabilities based on their potential impact and likelihood of exploitation, allowing for the prioritization of mitigation efforts.

At the core of expert-level protection is the utilization of advanced threat intelligence.

Experts continuously monitor the threat landscape to gather intelligence on emerging threats, vulnerabilities, and attack patterns.

This intelligence provides invaluable insights into the tactics employed by threat actors, enabling organizations to adapt their defenses accordingly.

Experts also leverage threat feeds, open-source intelligence, and collaborative information sharing to stay ahead of the curve.

A crucial aspect of advanced vulnerability protection is the integration of threat intelligence into security operations.

This involves the automation of threat detection and response mechanisms, allowing organizations to identify and mitigate threats in real-time.

Advanced security information and event management (SIEM) solutions, coupled with machine learning and artificial intelligence (AI), enable experts to detect anomalies and suspicious activities with precision.

They can respond swiftly to potential threats, minimizing the dwell time of attackers within their networks.

Furthermore, experts deploy advanced security orchestration and automation platforms to streamline incident response and remediation efforts.

These platforms enable rapid containment and eradication of threats, reducing the impact of attacks on an organization.

In addition to advanced technologies, expert-level protection techniques encompass a strong focus on the human element of cybersecurity.

Experts recognize that well-trained and vigilant employees are a critical line of defense against advanced threats.

They implement robust security awareness and training programs to educate staff about the latest threat trends and social engineering tactics.

Employees are encouraged to report suspicious activities promptly, fostering a culture of cybersecurity within the organization.

Phishing simulations and red team exercises are commonly used to assess the readiness of employees and fine-tune security awareness programs.

Furthermore, experts establish clear incident response plans and conduct regular tabletop exercises to ensure that all stakeholders are well-prepared to respond effectively in the event of a breach.

Encryption plays a pivotal role in expert-level vulnerability protection.

Experts employ encryption not only to secure data in transit but also to protect data at rest.

They utilize strong encryption algorithms and key management practices to ensure that sensitive information remains confidential, even if attackers gain access to it.

Moreover, experts implement robust access control measures, enforcing the principle of least privilege to limit exposure to potential vulnerabilities.

They leverage advanced identity and access management (IAM) solutions to enforce strict authentication and authorization policies.

Multi-factor authentication (MFA) and biometric authentication add additional layers of security to access control mechanisms.

In the realm of software development, experts promote secure coding practices as a foundational defense against vulnerabilities.

They conduct rigorous code reviews and employ automated static and dynamic code analysis tools to identify and remediate vulnerabilities within software applications.

Experts advocate for the adoption of secure development frameworks, emphasizing the importance of building security into the development lifecycle from the outset.

To bolster their defenses against advanced vulnerabilities, organizations often engage in penetration testing and red teaming exercises.

Experts simulate real-world attack scenarios to identify weaknesses in their security posture.

These exercises provide valuable insights into potential vulnerabilities that might be exploited by malicious actors.

The findings are used to refine security controls and remediation strategies.

Moreover, experts actively participate in collaborative threat-sharing communities and information-sharing partnerships with industry peers and government agencies.

These collaborative efforts enhance their visibility into emerging threats and enable the timely dissemination of threat intelligence.

This collective approach strengthens the overall cybersecurity posture of the organization.

Expert practitioners of vulnerability protection are also well-versed in the art of responsible disclosure.

When they discover vulnerabilities, they follow ethical guidelines to report them to the affected vendors and coordinate the release of patches or mitigations.

This responsible approach helps protect users and organizations while maintaining trust within the cybersecurity community.

In summary, expert techniques for protecting against advanced vulnerabilities encompass proactive defense strategies, advanced threat intelligence, integration of technology and human elements, encryption, access control, secure coding practices, penetration testing, and responsible disclosure.

These techniques represent the highest level of expertise in the field of cybersecurity and are essential for organizations seeking to defend against the most sophisticated cyber threats.

Conclusion

In the world of cybersecurity, knowledge is power, and the journey from a novice to an expert is both challenging and rewarding. The book bundle "ZERO DAY: Novice No More" takes readers on an educational voyage through the intricate landscape of software vulnerabilities and bug elimination. With four comprehensive books, this bundle equips readers with the skills and insights needed to tackle the most complex security challenges.

In "ZERO DAY DEMYSTIFIED: A Beginner's Guide to Uncovering Software Vulnerabilities" (Book 1), readers embark on their initial steps into the realm of vulnerability discovery. This book provides a solid foundation, demystifying the terminology and concepts surrounding software vulnerabilities. Novices are guided through the fundamental techniques for identifying and understanding these vulnerabilities, setting the stage for their journey towards becoming experts.

"ZERO DAY EXPOSED: Intermediate Techniques for Identifying and Patching Software Bugs" (Book 2) takes readers to the next level. Intermediate practitioners learn how to dig deeper, employing more advanced techniques to uncover vulnerabilities lurking within software. The book emphasizes the importance of proactive defense, helping readers identify and patch bugs before they can be exploited by malicious actors.

As readers progress further, "MASTERING ZERO DAY: Advanced Strategies for Vulnerability Discovery and

Remediation" (Book 3) becomes their trusted companion. In this advanced guide, readers explore cutting-edge strategies and methodologies for vulnerability discovery and remediation. Experts share their insights, ensuring that readers are well-prepared to address even the most sophisticated software vulnerabilities.

The journey culminates in "ZERO DAY UNLEASHED: Expert-Level Tactics for Exploiting and Protecting Against Software Vulnerabilities" (Book 4). This book delves into the intricate world of zero-day vulnerabilities, teaching readers both offensive and defensive strategies. Experts reveal the techniques used by threat actors to exploit vulnerabilities, empowering readers to understand, mitigate, and protect against these advanced threats.

As readers reach the end of this book bundle, they will have transformed from novices into proficient practitioners. They will possess the knowledge, skills, and confidence to navigate the ever-evolving landscape of software vulnerabilities and bug elimination. Armed with the insights gained from each book in this bundle, they are well-equipped to protect their organizations and contribute to the broader cybersecurity community.

"ZERO DAY: Novice No More" is not just a collection of books; it's a transformative learning experience. It empowers readers to take control of their cybersecurity journey, ensuring that they are no longer novices but experts in the critical field of software vulnerability discovery and mitigation.